T0106022

A Perfect Life

The Story of Swami Muktananda Paramahamsa

by Margaret Simpson

A SIDDHA YOGA PUBLICATION
PUBLISHED BY SYDA FOUNDATION

I knew even as a child that God was the most valuable being and that there was nothing like being friends with Him. I knew that God was the greatest and most dependable friend and He would always stand by you. I wanted to make friends with Him, but I was told that it was very difficult. So I set out in search of someone who was a friend of God, with whom I could become friends. I finally encountered the supreme Friend's friend, and he enabled me to be friends with his Friend. And now instead of seeking friends in this world, the best thing for me to do is to make people His friends.

— SWAMI MUKTANANDA

Published by SYDA Foundation
371 Brickman Rd., P.O. Box 600, South Fallsburg, NY 12779-0600, USA

ACKNOWLEDGMENTS
Many people helped prepare this book for publication. Heartfelt gratitude goes to
Margaret Simpson for her excellent adaptation and retelling of this inspiring life story;
to Josephine Taylor for her cover illustration and the full page illustrations and cameos of the
saints and Siddhas; to Melanie Hall for the vignette and spot illustrations; to Shane Conroy
for illustration direction; to Marjorie Corbett for her calligraphy; and to Michael Stewart
for creating the design. Editorial assistance was offered by Hemananda, Manuela Soares,
Carolyn Vaughan, Diane Fast, and Cynthia Kline. Christine McNally oversaw the editorial,
design, and production stages, and many others contributed their skills with willing and
loving hearts. Many thanks to them all.

– Kathy Morgan, editor

Copyright © 1996 SYDA Foundation.® All rights reserved

No part of this book may be reproduced or transmitted in any form
or by any means electronic or mechanical, including photocopy, recording,
or any information storage and retrieval system, without permission in writing
from SYDA Foundation, Permissions Department, 371 Brickman Rd.,
P.O. Box 600, South Fallsburg, NY 12779-0600, USA.

(Swami) MUKTANANDA, (Swami) CHIDVILASANANDA, GURUMAYI, SIDDHA YOGA,
and SIDDHA MEDITATION are registered trademarks of SYDA Foundation.®

First published 1996
Printed in the United States of America
00 99 98 97 96   5 4 3 2 1

Library of Congress Cataloging-in-Publication Data
Simpson, Margaret, 1943–
    A perfect life : the story of Swami Muktananda Paramahamsa / by Margaret Simpson.
      p. cm.
    Summary: Tells how a devout young boy from a small village in the south of India grew
to be the spiritual leader of many people around the world.
    ISBN 0-911307-49-4
    1. Muktananda, Swami, 1908–   —Juvenile literature. 2. Hindus—India—Biography—
Juvenile literature. [1. Muktananda, Swami, 1908–   . 2. Hindus—India.]
BL1175.M77S67 1996
294.5'092 — dc20
[B]   96-27221
                                                                         CIP
                                                                          AC

Contents

A NOTE ON THE TEXT

Most Indian languages are written in an alphabet called Devanagari. It looks very different from the Roman alphabet that English is written in, so in order to read these words, they are transliterated, or changed into the Roman alphabet. If a word from an Indian language is well known or if it usually appears in English dictionaries, it is not italicized in the text and no pronunciation guide appears in the glossary. Less common Indian language words appear in italic, and long vowels for the Sanskrit words are indicated by a bar over the vowel. For more information on long and short vowels and on pronouncing these words, please see the pronunciation guide preceding the glossary.

Introduction

The book you are holding in your hands traces the life of an extraordinary being. The story starts with a boy who, at a very young age, realizes he wants to know God more than he wants anything else on earth. With this goal in mind, he sets out on incredible adventures filled with amazing people, beautiful and fantastic places, tests of courage and strength, and challenges of every kind. The story is spellbinding, like any great tale, but what makes this story so amazing is that it is true, and that the life it traces has magically touched so many people — people like you and me.

I met Swami Muktananda twenty-two years ago, when I was only two years old. I don't even remember that first meeting, but I know that it was one of the most important days of my life. Since then I have grown up receiving the incredible gifts that Baba, as we knew him, and now Gurumayi Chidvilasananda have showered upon me and upon anyone who is ready and willing to receive them.

"What are these gifts?" you wonder. The gifts that a perfected being, a Guru like Baba, gives come in countless forms. Whatever form it takes, the Guru gives us what we need when we need it. For example, when I was in the fourth grade, Baba had an amazing way of teaching the kids in Gurudev Siddha Peeth, the ashram in Ganeshpuri, India, about the discipline and attention that you needed to do well in school. Just after breakfast every morning all of the kids would go to the Nityananda temple and take their seats. Our first class was chanting the *Rudram* and the teacher was none other than Baba. He would come into the temple, sit down, and chant the whole *Rudram* with us. Even though we were just young children, Baba placed great importance on being with us for that time every morning. He taught us about posture, which helped us to sit more comfortably. He taught us the correct pronunciation of the Sanskrit syllables. And at the end of the chant, Baba would give us each a chocolate as *prasād* and send us off to school. I wasn't thinking about it at the time, but what Baba was doing was not just teaching us how to sing the *Rudram,* he was not just giving us chocolates, he was not just laughing and joking with us, he was teaching us how to be students. When I was finishing my senior year at Dartmouth College in New Hampshire, I was thankful Baba had taught me the discipline that gave me the strength to do well in school.

As I went through middle school and then high school and college, I realized more and more how much I had received from Baba and Gurumayi. I often didn't recognize these gifts until they were pointed out by others. Sometimes teachers or coaches wondered how I stayed focused and didn't get flustered. I realized that when I was about to get nervous before a test or before a ski race, I silently repeated the mantra *Om Namah Shivāya* to stay focused and calm. As I grew up and people told me that I was very easy to get along with, I started to see for myself that Baba's teaching, "See God In Each Other," made it very easy and comfortable to relate to other people. When I was challenged in school or at work, I recognized that the place I drew strength from was the place inside me where all the power of creation is available to us. Baba and Gurumayi's ultimate gift is taking us to that place inside so that eventually we may live in that state forever.

As a young child it seemed so natural to have Baba in my life. After all, when I was four years old I did not think about Baba as a Guru or as a spiritual master. I thought about him more like an uncle—an uncle who was loving and playful, who let my sister and me ride on his elephant, and who taught me how to play the drum. Now as a twenty-four year old starting a small business, I still think about Baba as my loving uncle, but I also understand that my contact with him was an extraordinary blessing. Everything Baba did had a single divine purpose. His purpose was to lead people toward God and to show them that they can live in complete peace and happiness. His purpose was to uplift the world by uplifting people everywhere.

I am one of the fortunate people who was lucky enough to spend time with Baba Muktananda. His teachings, his love, and his nurturing shaped me into the person I am today, and they still help me grow. Baba had so much to offer, and his giving has never stopped. You, too, are touched by Baba's life. His work of uplifting the world continues through Gurumayi. Like Baba, she showers all of us with love, with teachings of righteousness, and with the sublime gift of the knowledge that God is alive inside each of us. Everything that Gurumayi gives us is a continuation of Baba Muktananda's life. So begin reading and watch how an adventurous young boy in India found his way into your life.

Stephen Mullennix
Los Angeles, California
March, 1996

A Boon from God

This story begins in the early years of the twentieth century, in a small village in the south of India. The village was called Dharmasthala, and it was home to a young couple, who, at first glance, appeared to have everything in the world that anyone could possibly want. They were both healthy. They lived with their two young daughters in a large, cool house overlooking a fine estate on the banks of the Netravati River near Mangalore. Materially, they wanted for nothing, and the wife especially knew that the secret of a contented life lay in putting God first. And yet, like many people before them, this young couple found that it wasn't always so easy to accept the will of God. For, after the birth of their daughters, years went by and there was no sign of a son. Sons were very important in India, especially at that time, and especially to landowners. Daughters left home when they married. Without a son, a couple would have no one to farm the land when the husband's strength failed him, and no one to take care of them in their old age.

Near the village of Dharmasthala there was a temple to Lord Manjunath, which is one of the names of Lord Shiva. The young woman knew how disappointed her husband was that she had not borne a son. She decided to go to the temple to pray again to Lord Manjunath for the son they both longed for. She bathed and dressed herself in a fine sari. She took garlands and coconuts as gifts. And when she reached the temple, she prayed, humbly, from the depth of her great longing. "Lord, you have given my husband and me so many blessings. I thank you for your goodness from the bottom of my heart. But there is one boon, Lord, I beg from you. Give us another child, Lord. And this time, please, please, bless us with a son."

A few days later, she was quietly cleaning rice when her servant told her that a man was at the door.

"Who is it?" she asked.

"I don't know. A *sādhu*."

"Give him food," said the young wife. *Sādhus* were people who had given up everything—home, family, trade, profession—in order to devote their whole lives to the search for God. They owned nothing and wandered from place to place, temple to temple, relying on God's grace and the goodness of others for their food and shelter. The young woman and her husband were always generous to *sādhus*. Having so much themselves, they saw it as their duty to give to these devout seekers. This one, it seemed, was not asking for food.

"Mata, he wishes to speak personally. To you," said the servant.

The woman rose and went out to the terrace. There stood a thin *sādhu* whom she had never seen before. She stooped and touched the ground at his feet as a mark of respect.

"You wish to speak with me?" she asked.

The *sādhu* nodded. "Your prayer," he said.

"Yes?" An electric feeling of anticipation ran through the woman's body.

"So that it may be answered, I have been sent to give you a holy mantra. If you repeat this mantra, you will have the son you desire."

"What is it?" whispered the woman.

"Five syllables," said the man. "*Namah Shivāya.*"

"I know it," said the woman, almost disappointed. "*Om Namah Shivāya.* I honor the Lord dwelling within me."

The *sādhu* nodded. "You know it, but have you really understood what it means?" he asked. "*Om Namah Shivāya* is a great mantra. A mantra so great it has the power to create the universe. Remember that when you repeat it. Repeat it with great concentration. The Lord will grant you your boon."

The woman thanked him. She went back into the house to fetch some rice and *dal* for the *sādhu,* all the while wondering who

he was. How did he know about her prayer, and was it really true that this mantra which she had known all her life was going to help her to bear the son she longed for? By the time she came back, he was gone.

At first the woman said nothing to her husband. She did not want to raise his hopes in case the mantra did not work after all, but she herself was full of hope. She did what the *sādhu* said. She repeated the mantra ceaselessly to herself—when she sat in the family temple to meditate, before she went to sleep at night, when she served her husband his meals, as she went about her daily tasks around the house, even when family and friends came to visit and she was surrounded by chattering visitors. As she repeated it, she began to forget the obsessive longing that came between her and happiness. The ache in her heart eased. Soon she found that the mantra was there all the time, even when her mind seemed to have forgotten it, repeating itself as regularly as her breathing. Some days, when the mantra was skimming along inside her, and she thought that in some way she had become the mantra, or perhaps the mantra had become her, the *sādhu's* words would come back to her. "A mantra so great it has the power to create the universe"—that was what he had said. Then she would marvel at the power of the words she had been given—the power of creation itself!

Soon she could sense a new life inside of her. She hardly dared hope when she felt the first tiny flutters that were the baby's shifting limbs, but later when the kicks were big and strong, she thought it must be the boy she and her husband longed for.

The baby was born on May 16, 1908. Dawn was just breaking, and a full moon was still visible in the lightening sky. The young wife went out into the compound. There, as she sat cleaning her teeth with a twig in the first rays of the sun, her baby was born, very easily and with almost no warning. And, to her joy, it was a boy! A fine healthy boy! He was so beautiful, so adorable, his parents called him Krishna, because Krishna is the name given to God in his most lovable aspect. Her husband was so pleased and grateful that they at last had a son that he laid the newborn baby on a set of scales and put an equal weight of gold and silver on the other side. Together the little family went back to the temple of Lord Manjunath, where Krishna's father gave the gold and silver as a thank-you offering to Lord Shiva.

The Eldest Son

Krishna grew up a bright, quick, alert child, interested in everything. He was doted on by his mother and his two older sisters. He followed them to the well and watched them draw up clean cold water. He tried to help them carry it to the house and watched them transfer it to cooking pots in the kitchen, or to the big brass pots that stood in the bathroom, ready for his father to take a bath whenever he came in from his work on the estate. Sometimes his father might take Krishna with him as he went to inspect his rice fields or to check on the coconut crop. At other times he took the boy with him to the village. Sometimes the men gathered there for local trials of strength. Krishna's father very often won these. It was said that he was so strong he could lift an ox!

Krishna was strong like his father. He was never one to pick a quarrel, but he was a brave boy, and if anyone challenged him he gave as good as he got. He was afraid of nothing and no one.

From both his parents, Krishna inherited a great love for God. His mother never forgot the visit of the *sādhu*. She had repeated *Om Namah Shivāya* as she carried Krishna in her womb. She repeated it to him the day he was born. She repeated it as she fed him and bathed him and rocked him to sleep. As soon as he could talk, Krishna was repeating it, too. As he grew older, he said *Om Namah Shivāya* eleven times before eating his food, and if ever he forgot his mother would catch his hand in midair.

"First say your mantra, then eat your food," she would remind him.

From the time he was a tiny child, Krishna loved stories. There was no electricity in those days, and no television, so families and friends gathered together at night to hear all the well-known stories of the Indian gods and saints read aloud by the light of a paraffin lamp.

Sitting there in the shadowy darkness, little Krishna listened spellbound as he heard how the wicked demon Ravana kidnapped Lord Rama's wife, Sita, and how Hanuman, the monkey god, helped Lord Rama to rescue her with an army of monkeys. His eyes widened when he heard how, in anger, Lord Shiva had cut off the head of Parvati's son, Ganesh. He was relieved when Parvati persuaded her husband to restore the boy to life with another head. He wondered how he would feel if he had an elephant's head. Lord Ganesh didn't seem to mind. He was playful and full of fun and came to be known as the remover of obstacles.

As he grew older, it was the stories of the child-saints that Krishna loved best.

One of his favorites was the story of Prahlad. Prahlad's father was a demon king who didn't believe in God. He thought he was the greatest living creature. When he discovered that his son repeated the name of God all the time because he thought God was greater than his father, he became very, very angry. He tried everything he could think of to make Prahlad stop, but nothing worked. Finally, he ordered his men to build a huge pyre and told Prahlad that unless he stopped his nonsense he would put him in the middle of it and set it alight. Prahlad took no notice. His father was always threatening him with dreadful things. He went on calmly repeating the name of God. This made Prahlad's father angrier than ever.

"You think I don't mean it? I'll show you," he said. He gestured to the palace guards, who grabbed Prahlad and tied him to a stake in the middle of the pyre. Another guard carried a flaming torch and thrust it into the bottom of the pyre. The wood was dry. It crackled and caught. Big yellow flames leapt up around him, but still Prahlad showed no fear. He just went on repeating the name of God. His father was dumbfounded.

"Look, the pyre is alight!" he shouted. "The pyre is alight! You fool! How do you think the name of God is going to help you now?"

Prahlad wasn't upset. "Father, can't you understand? One who repeats the name of God knows no fear. Neither earth, nor fire, nor air, nor any other element can frighten him. To you it may appear that I am surrounded by leaping flames, yet thanks to the name of God, it feels to me as if a cool breeze is blowing on my body."

"You won't say that when the fire gets hotter," shouted Prahlad's cruel father. "More wood!" he yelled to the guards.

The guards threw more wood on the flames. The fire burned redder and hotter. Yet, miraculously, Prahlad still appeared to be unharmed.

"He's not burning! Why aren't you burning?" shouted the exasperated king.

"Father, to burn you need anger, and I have no anger," said Prahlad.

Prahlad's father and the guards watched amazed as Prahlad sat in the fire repeating the name of God until he went into a state of deep meditation. Around him the fire changed from leaping flames to red-hot embers, then to grey-white ashes. Then, finally it died. Prahlad was still alive, still deep in meditation. God had protected him.

When Krishna got together with his friends, he soon had them all play-acting stories like these, although of course they were much too sensible to try anything silly with real fire. They would get clay and pretend it was sacred ash and smear it on their bodies. They would play at being yogis and *sādhus* or great beings who could perform miracles. For his friends, this was just make-believe, but for Krishna it was something much more important. He knew that when great beings said, "This shall happen," it did. And he wondered if he could be such a being when he grew up.

There was one time of year that was especially good for stories. This was the festival of Navaratri, when the harvest was in, and troupes of traveling players arrived in the village. Then there would be great excitement as they built a makeshift stage beside the temple and put up awnings and tents all around. On the night of the performance, everyone from the village would gather to see the show. The rich people sat in the temple and everyone else crowded under the awnings. The stage was brightly lit by hurricane lamps as the actors, their faces painted like masks, leapt onto the stage. There were clowns, and jokes, and songs, and music.

There were lights and smoke and other magical effects. Now the stories of gods and saints, heros and villains really came alive. These stories were well known. They came from ancient epics like the *Rāmāyana* or the *Mahābhārata*, but the actors always gave them a modern twist. Krishna watched spellbound as Yudhishthira gambled his kingdom away. He was shocked when the wicked Kauravas tried to strip Draupadi of her sari, and he laughed with relief when they couldn't because the cloth kept on coming and coming and coming. He saw how his namesake, Lord Krishna, helped Arjuna by darkening the sun at the crucial moment in the

great battle. No doubt about it, the gods and great beings were powerful.

After the actors had packed up their tents and moved on, Krishna and his friends would perform the stories in the school playground just as they had seen the actors do. Very often Krishna was the director, telling the others what to do, but he liked acting, too, especially if he could play his namesake, Lord Krishna, or the sage Narada. He loved playing the god, the sage, or the *sādhu*.

At home and in the school playground, Krishna led a happy life. In the classroom it was a different story. In those days even very young children had to learn by heart strings of facts and dates and long boring poems. Sometimes these poems weren't even in their own language. Because India was ruled by the British at this time, Indian schoolboys had to learn poems in English, just like British schoolboys. It didn't matter whether they understood what they were saying, only whether they had memorized it correctly. Krishna was a clever boy. He could do this easily, when he put his mind to it. The only trouble was, he didn't always put his mind to it. To him, this sort of learning seemed pointless. There were far more interesting things to be seen looking out of the classroom window. In fact, his interest in what was going on outside the window sometimes got Krishna into trouble. When he was grown up, he used to tell the story of how, one day, during a math lesson, he watched a snake glide into a hole in a tree in the school yard. He became so absorbed in watching it that he stopped listening to the teacher explaining the rules of long division. Next thing he knew the teacher was standing right over him.

"Did you hear me, Krishna?"

Krishna jumped. "Yes, sir."

"Well?" said the teacher. "Answer. Is there anything left over?"

Krishna thought he was talking about the snake. "Only the tail, sir," he said.

All the boys in the class tittered, but his teacher wasn't smiling. It was then that Krishna realized that the teacher was talking about the lesson on the blackboard. He was in trouble!

Who Am I?

Krishna's curiosity about everything around him—nature, people, mechanical things—would stay with him all his life. He was fascinated by the laws of science and nature and by why people behaved as they did. Yet at the same time, he sensed that there were much more important questions for a human being. Questions like "Who am I?" "Why was I born?" and "Where am I going?"

Krishna never doubted that the answers to such questions lay in devotion to God. He could see that in his favorite stories of the child-saints. Prahlad had been so sure of God that his faith had saved him from the flames. And there was another child-saint, Dhruva, who had given up everything in order to know God— food, water, even air!

Dhruva was the eldest son of a king who had two wives. The second wife, his stepmother, didn't like Dhruva much. She was jealous because he would be king one day, while her son would never be king. She was unkind to Dhruva and told him he could not sit on his father's lap. His father did not want to quarrel with his new wife and did nothing to help him. So Dhruva, who was only a little boy, went crying to his mother.

His mother was sad to see her son so unhappy, but she was out of favor with her husband and knew there was nothing she could do.

"The only thing you can do is go and ask the help of Lord Vishnu," she told her son. "Maybe he can make your father see the error of his ways."

Dhruva decided he would do just that. He was only five years old, and he didn't know where Lord Vishnu lived, but he knew there were some sacred woods nearby where many sages and *sādhus* lived. He decided he would go there and ask them. When the sages saw him, they weren't very kind. They laughed at him. How could a tiny five-year-old find the Lord God when they had spent all their lives looking? Only the great sage Narada took the child seriously. He gave Dhruva a mantra and sent him to a sacred place by the river Yamuna. There the child stayed, willing Lord Vishnu to appear so

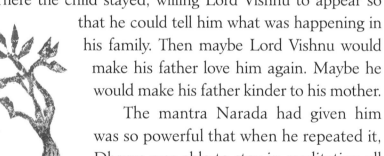

that he could tell him what was happening in his family. Then maybe Lord Vishnu would make his father love him again. Maybe he would make his father kinder to his mother.

The mantra Narada had given him was so powerful that when he repeated it, Dhruva was able to stay in meditation all day long except when he went to gather berries for food. There was no sign of Lord Vishnu, however, so Dhruva decided it was because he was wasting time gathering berries. He stopped eating and drank only water. A month later, there was still no sign of Lord Vishnu, so he decided to live on air. And when Lord Vishnu still did not appear, Dhruva stopped breathing.

As his breath stopped moving, so did all the air throughout the universe. At this, gods and men alike became terrified. They prayed to Lord Vishnu to intervene before the power of Dhruva's longing destroyed all of creation.

Dhruva, meanwhile, was still deep in peaceful meditation. He felt someone gently touch his cheek. He opened his eyes and saw before him Lord Vishnu, alive in all his light and love and splendor. Feelings of pure ecstasy flooded through Dhruva's body, and in that moment, he knew that his father's love was a tiny, tiny thing to ask for. What he should have been seeking was to rest in the happiness he felt now, the happiness of being in the presence of God. Lord Vishnu knew what Dhruva was feeling. He looked at him with great compassion.

"You have learned a great lesson. You have learned that to ask God for anything other than to know Him is to pray for illusion. Yet because you trusted God, you have drawn grace, which has brought you to right understanding. You should teach this lesson to others."

Then he told Dhruva to go home to fulfill his earthly destiny. When Dhruva arrived, he received a great welcome from his father, his mother, his stepmother, and the rest of the family. Not long afterward, his father renounced his crown in order to seek God, and Dhruva became a strong and just king, who ruled his kingdom for thirty thousand years. At the end of that time the Lord made him immortal and set him in the sky as the Pole Star, the still star of the northern hemisphere by which sailors set their compasses.

Dhruva's determination to find God made a deep impression on the young Krishna. He, too, wanted to find God. God was clearly the greatest and most dependable being in the world, and so the most important thing in the world was to be friends with Him. Nothing else mattered. The more Krishna thought about it, the more obvious it became that in order to become friends with God, he had to find someone, as Dhruva had found Narada, who was already friends with God and who could guide him to Him.

In fact, he already knew someone who he thought might be that friend of God. He was a *sādhu*. His name was Nityananda Baba, and he used to pass through Krishna's village from time to time. He was very tall, and his skin was dark and gleaming as if there were a sheen to it. He didn't wear clothes like other people. The most he wore was a loincloth and occasionally a shawl or blanket around his shoulders.

There were lots of stories told about Nityananda Baba. It was said that he had been born a saint, but that he underwent hard-ships and difficult spiritual practices in order to inspire others. He had lived for a long time in a cave in the middle of a forest quite near where Krishna lived, and because there was no natural water supply nearby, it was said he had created a stream of water within the cave itself. He was fond of beautiful gardens and had planted coconut palms and mango trees around the cave. Now he wan-dered from place to place on foot, and people said that he could move as fast as the mind itself.

Krishna always loved it when Nityananda Baba visited the village. Just seeing the *sādhu* made him feel blessed and happy. In fact, whenever Nityananda Baba was seen nearing the village, Krishna and his friends would rush out from their classrooms to run after him. As soon as he saw them coming, Nityananda Baba, who loved playing with children, would run away from them yelling. The children would yell, too, and rush after him. Then he would climb a tree and sit on a branch out of their reach while all the children gathered beneath.

As he reached his teenage years, Krishna found he was thinking about Nityananda Baba more and more. Here was someone who actually lived the life that Krishna played and dreamed about. He wandered about the country, unburdened by possessions. Krishna wondered what it would be like to leave home and family and not know where the next meal was coming from or where you were going to sleep that night. He wondered if he could live the way Nityananda Baba did.

Not long after he started having such thoughts, Nityananda Baba appeared in the school playground. This time, when the children came rushing after him, there was no yelling and running. Instead, he let the children gather around him, and then he beckoned Krishna out of the crowd of boys. He put his arm around him and stroked his cheeks for a minute or two. Then, quite suddenly, he walked away. For the rest of his life, Krishna never forgot the sight of his retreating figure. He never forgot how fast he moved. It seemed as if his feet weren't touching the ground.

That meeting left Krishna profoundly changed. Now when he sat at his school desk, thoughts of Nityananda filled his mind. He remembered Nityananda's big gentle hands stroking his face—hands that carried nothing as he walked away. No books, no clothes, no papers, no suitcase. He remembered the lightness of his walk. He remembered the sheen of his skin. He thought about his name. He knew *nitya* meant "eternal" and *ānanda* meant "bliss." So Nityananda would mean "the bliss of the eternal." Krishna wondered what that really meant. Everything that lived would die one day, so what was it that was eternal?

Now when he went home, he looked at his father, so strong, honorable, hardworking, and his mother, so devoted to God and to her family. He looked around the comfortable house where he had spent his childhood and the estate that everyone assumed he would inherit when he grew up. Already, he knew, his parents must be thinking about whom he should marry.

To Krishna these things seemed unimportant. They were passing, not eternal. What was important was to be friends with God. To know God. That had to come before everything else. And it seemed to him, then—he was fifteen years old—that you couldn't really do that if your mind was busy with crops and money and family obligations. Krishna loved his parents, and he didn't want to hurt them, but he knew he wasn't going to live the life they had planned for him. He was going to walk through the world unburdened, like Nityananda. He was going to become as firm in his faith and spiritual practice as Prahlad and Dhruva. He was going to know God.

As the days passed, this longing to know God became like a fire inside him. He was absolutely certain in his own mind of what he had to do. And one morning, without telling his parents, he walked out of his home never to return. He took off his school clothes, wrapped them in a bundle, and threw them over the garden wall. Instead of going to school, he took the road out of town that led to the hills. Much later he would write to his parents to tell them he was safe, and they should not worry, but for that day, and the days that followed, he only knew that he was doing what he had to do. He was free. He was a *sādhu*. He had no money, and he didn't really know where he was going, but for some reason he felt fine about it. He was giving his life to God, and he knew God would look after him and show him what to do next.

The Young Seeker

There weren't many cars about in those days, and still fewer trucks, so Krishna traveled barefoot on dirt roads, wearing only a length of cloth called a *lungi* wrapped round his waist. He headed for the town of Hubli, because someone had told him there was an ashram there famous for its discipline and learning, from which no traveler was ever turned away without food. It was the ashram of Siddharudha Swami.

Krishna arrived in Hubli and asked for directions to the ashram. He knew he was nearing the right place when he heard a welcome and familiar sound. It was the mantra his mother had taught him, *Om Namah Shivāya*, being chanted by scores of voices. The sound of this chant echoed through the ashram day and night. In addition, every morning and evening there was *satsang*—the coming together, to chant and to meditate, of people who loved and longed for God. There were always discussions going on among the great thinkers and teachers of the region.

India

•*Hubli*

Mangalore •

The Guru whose ashram it was, Siddharudha Swami, was a remarkable being in every way. He was over seven feet tall, and on special occasions he would dress in silk, embroidered with gold thread, and wear a crown set with precious jewels. Yet fine clothes did not really matter to him, and much of the time he wore nothing but a loincloth. He was a great being, one who lived in a state of oneness with God, and yet he was kind, practical, and down-to-earth. His ashram fed hundreds of people every day. When seekers complained to Siddharudha Swami that they could not concentrate on God because they had to take care of their families, Siddharudha showed them the rows and rows of cooking stoves in the ashram kitchens and told them that he had a larger family than any of them. It didn't stop him from knowing God.

Krishna asked Siddharudha Swami to accept him as a student in his ashram, and Siddharudha, seeing a boy of great intelligence and exceptional longing, said yes. There, in Siddharudha's ashram, Krishna was taught the philosophy of Vedanta. The word *philosophy* means "the love, study, and pursuit of wisdom." Vedanta contains the ideas of the ancient Indian scriptures known as the Vedas. Many of these ideas are very subtle, but because they were taught in a way that connected with his everyday experience, they became real and meaningful to Krishna. Here study made sense to him, because it was about God and how to know Him. It connected with his inner longing.

One of his teachers at this time was Kabirdas, a great disciple of Siddharudha's, who had been a prince before he became a monk. Kabirdas taught Krishna in the same way that the forest sagès in ancient times had passed on their understanding to their disciples. First he recited a mantra to Krishna and then asked him if he had understood it.

"I heard it," said Krishna.

Kabirdas shook his head. "I am asking, have you understood it?"

Krishna said nothing.

"I have repeated this mantra which says that the Self is you," persisted Kabirdas. "Have you understood it?"

"I have understood about the Knower," said Krishna.

"Who is the Knower? How does He know?"

"You are the teacher," said Krishna. "You explain it."

Kabirdas gave him a candy. "Eat it," he said. And when Krishna had eaten it he said, "Well? How was it?"

"It was very sweet," said Krishna.

"Who knows it was sweet?" asked Kabirdas.

"Somebody," said Krishna.

"That Somebody is the Knower," said Kabirdas. "And the Knower is the Self."

Krishna thought about this. As he did so, one of the great truths of Vedanta came alive for him: that we are not our thoughts, or feelings, or sensations. We are the One who knows our thoughts, feelings, and sensations. He began to understand that this part of us, which is called the Knower, or the Witness, or the Self, is beyond everything. No matter what happens in our lives, the Self is unchanging. The Self is eternal.

It was while he was living at Siddharudha Swami's ashram that Krishna became a monk, or *sannyāsi*. A *sannyāsi* is one who gives up worldly things in order to dedicate his life completely to God. In a series of solemn ceremonies he dies to his former life. Now he no longer belongs to any particular family or country, and he promises to form no new attachments. To symbolize his break with the past he is given a new name, and he has the understanding "I am no longer this individual body. I am one with the entire universe." He prays, "O Lord, I give refuge to all creatures. Now you must give refuge to me." From now on he dresses in orange robes to remind himself and everyone else that he has given up everything that most people hold dear.

The name that Krishna was given at his *sannyāsa* ceremony was Muktananda, which means the "bliss of liberation." From then on, for the rest of his life, Krishna was no more. Instead he was known as Swami Muktananda.

Siddharudha Swami sent the young Swami Muktananda to the ashram of another of his disciples, Muppinarya Swami, who was a great scholar. At his ashram, Swami Muktananda completed a five-year course of study. He also mastered many practical skills. For instance, he was put in charge of building a temple, and as a result learned a great deal about engineering and architecture, which stood him in good stead years later when he had his own ashram.

Siddharudha also sent Muktananda to stay with Mallikarjuna Swami, who was renowned, among other things, for the amount of food he could eat. The young Muktananda had never seen anyone eat so much. He wasn't fat so where did he put it all? It seemed as if he had hollow legs! Watching him eat, Muktananda realized his teachers were right when they spoke about the need for good food when you were meditating a lot. Mallikarjuna's huge meals were all being digested in the fire of yoga.

Mallikarjuna Swami gave the young swami his first lessons in Kashmir Shaivism, another branch of Indian philosophy which, later in his life, was to become as important to him as Vedanta. Shaivism teaches that God is not just the Witness. God is everything. Tastes and smells, thoughts and feelings, good people and bad—God expresses Himself as all of them. There is nothing and nowhere in the entire universe where God is not.

Six years went by, with Muktananda living in ashrams in and around Hubli. During this time, Siddharudha Swami, who was an old man, came to the end of his life in his physical body. He had been a very great being and Muktananda had loved him very much. He missed him. When he had completed his studies with Muppinarya, he decided the time had come to seek out other saints and great beings. He left Hubli and took to the road again with nothing but the clothes on his back, a water jug, and a stick to walk with.

The Wandering Sadhu

In the years that followed, Swami Muktananda covered thousands of miles on foot, walking along railway lines, sleeping under bridges. He traveled the length and breadth of India, not once, but three times. Although there were more cars and trucks with every year that passed, he almost never hitchhiked because he preferred to walk in the open air. He would eat only if people offered him food. He never begged. So if no one gave him anything to eat, he went hungry. Once he was so hungry that he mixed dirt with water and ate that. Sometimes he was so cold at night that he would use a shroud to cover himself till morning. It was a hard life, yet he loved the freedom of the road and the open sky. Later he said how much he had enjoyed being a pilgrim, wandering from shrine to shrine, with no worries.

He became very hardy living outdoors through all the extremes of blazing sun and bitter cold and driving monsoon rain. Sometimes he suffered the terrible stomach cramps of dysentery; sometimes he shivered and shook with malaria. But he was young, and tough, and consumed with his longing to know God. "No disease can trouble a person who is already burning in the flames of the pain of separation from God," he once said. "All minor ailments are burnt up in that fire."

It was during these years that he mastered every single one of the postures of hatha yoga. These exercises made his body strong and supple and helped him to sit for long periods of meditation. He learned Ayurvedic medicine, the Indian system for preventing and treating disease. He learned to cook, gathering recipes from many places and people throughout India. He also learned martial arts in order to protect himself. He had to. He met some tough customers in the course of his travels, and he carried the scars to prove it. He also met every other sort of person there is—householders and scholars, soldiers and merchants, con men and thieves. He learned something about human nature from all of them.

Some of the strangest people he met on his travels were saints. There was one called Athani Shiva Yogi, who never allowed any of his disciples or followers anywhere near him. Instead he lived all by himself inside a big circle of rocks. If anyone tried to come near, he would reach for a rock and hurl it.

Even though he was so odd, people said that Athani Shiva Yogi had real understanding, and so Swami Muktananda decided to go to visit him.

"Don't go!" said the nearby villagers. "He'll throw rocks at you! And he has a good aim!"

"So what?" said Swami Muktananda.

"The rocks will hit me, not you. Leave me alone to do what I want." And he walked out of the village in the direction of Athani Shiva Yogi's homemade fortress.

He approached very slowly and cautiously. Athani Shiva Yogi watched him over his wall of rocks. Although he didn't throw anything, he wasn't exactly friendly.

"What do you want?" he shouted.

"O Baba, I have come for a mantra," said the young swami.

There were no rocks flying through the air yet, so Swami Muktananda, still cautious, moved closer. When he got right up to the wall of rocks, Athani Shiva Yogi took off one of his shoes and laid it on a rock. It was a leather shoe with a toe that turned up.

"You want a mantra? Pick up that shoe and put it against your ear," he told Muktananda.

Swami Muktananda did so. To his amazement, he could hear the shoe repeating, "*Om Namah Shivāya, Om Namah Shivāya, Om Namah Shivāya.*"

"And now get out of here!" said Athani Shiva Yogi, picking up a rock.

Muktananda did so, as fast as he could. From this strange, reclusive yogi he had learned that if the person repeating the mantra has truly become one with the mantra, then everything he touches automatically starts to echo with the sound of that mantra. The only trouble was, he didn't know how you became one with the mantra.

Another encounter which affected the young swami profoundly was with a great yogi called Swami Lingananda in Kashi. Kashi is the name used in the scriptures for the city of Varanasi in the north of India, on the river Ganges. It is said if you die there you will not need to be reborn in another body. For this reason many people go there to die, and the city is famous for the funeral pyres that burn on the ghats of the riverbanks.

Swami Lingananda told Muktananda he should stay for three weeks with a *sādhu* who lived down by the burning ghats. It was a creepy place to be, especially at night, when the fires were dying and everyone had gone home. By day, small processions of people brought the bodies of their loved ones to be burnt. He watched the men who tended the fires throw bodies around like garbage. He heard them crackle in the fire. He saw them thrown into the river half-burnt, and the fish darting after them to feed. This experience made a deep impression on the mind of the young swami. From then on he never forgot that everything that lives must one day die, and that we never know when that day will be.

Swami Lingananda had other scary experiences in store for the young swami. He knew that Muktananda, at that time in his life, was obsessed with cleanliness and purity. He was reluctant to drink water served by anyone else or to eat their food. As a wandering *sādhu*, he depended on other people to give him food and drink, so this made life very difficult. Swami Lingananda thought of just the way to cure him. He asked Muktananda to help him prepare a feast. The young swami always liked to perform service for the people who helped him and so he willingly agreed.

A lot of people came to the feast, and they all enjoyed themselves. Then, toward the end, when most people had gone home, a lone late guest appeared. He was an old leper, with the ugly sores of his illness all over his mouth and crippled hands. Nowadays we know that leprosy is not very infectious, and in any case it can be treated with drugs, but in those days it was one of the most feared of all diseases. In every civilization throughout history lepers have been outcasts, who had to live apart from others in case they infected them.

None of this bothered Swami Lingananda, who welcomed the leper warmly. He told Swami Muktananda to feed the man with his own hands. Muktananda was horrified. He steeled himself to do as Lingananda had asked him. He fed the leper as fast as he could, making sure his fingers didn't go anywhere near the leper's lips. As a result, between them they spilled a lot of food. Finally, the ordeal was over. The leper had eaten enough, and he went on his way.

Lingananda took one look at all the food that had fallen on the ground and guessed what had happened. He told the young swami he should eat it up. Muktananda was aghast. It was all he could do to swallow one tiny bit of that food. Lingananda watched him and then swept up what remained in his own hands, savoring it as if there was nothing wrong and this was the most delicious food in the world. As he swallowed the last morsel, Lingananda smiled and wiped his lips.

"Did you notice how quickly that leper walked?" he asked.

Muktananda stared at him. Now that Lingananda mentioned it, the man had been walking fast for a sick man.

"No leper walks that fast," said Lingananda. "That was Lord Shiva himself in disguise. But it seems you couldn't take his *prasād*."

Bapumayi was another great being who liked to remind himself of the transience of life. He lived in a graveyard outside the town of Pandharpur, but every day he came into town and walked through the streets. As he did so, all the local shopkeepers used to give him money. One day Swami Muktananda followed him to see what he would do with it. Bapumayi looked over his shoulder and asked him why he was following him.

"I want to come to your home," replied the young swami.

"Why? You're a nice man," said Bapumayi. "And I belong to a low caste and live in a graveyard. You shouldn't come with me."

Swami Muktananda was not easily put off. He kept following Bapumayi. Soon they had left the city behind, and after a while they came to the graveyard, which was on the banks of a river. Bapumayi went right to the edge of the river and prayed.

"O Mother, keep this money with you," he said. "I have no place to keep it. You look after it." And with that, he threw all the money the shopkeepers had given him into the river and sat down peacefully beneath a tree. Muktananda knelt and touched Bapumayi's feet as a sign of respect.

Bapumayi shook his head. "You shouldn't do that," he said. "I belong to a low caste. You are a *sannyāsi*. When you took your vows, you became Narayana, the Lord Himself. Go and worship the statue of Lord Vitthal."

"I've done that," said Muktananda. "Now I'm seated before a real, live Vitthal."

Bapumayi protested some more. Then he stopped protesting and began to speak very softly.

"O swami, everything is the embodiment of God. There is nothing else. The Lord is above, below, to the left and right. You are that God. There is nothing else but Him. Chant His name with great ecstasy."

As he sought out all these different Siddhas, or perfected beings, Swami Muktananda confirmed what he had sensed ever since he first met Nityananda Baba. It wasn't what people said or did that made them great beings. It wasn't what they looked like. It was the state that they were in. Great beings were content because they were in touch with a place of ecstasy inside themselves. The place of ecstasy was called the Self. It was what the scriptures called "existence, consciousness, and bliss absolute."

When you knew That in yourself, you could also see it in everyone and everything around you. When that happened it no longer mattered whether you walked naked through the streets or wore a jeweled crown. You could run an ashram, or live in a graveyard. Nothing affected your state. You were completely free.

How did you get into that state, though? Despite the name he had been given, despite all his studying and all his meditation practice, despite having been in the presence of so many great Siddhas, Swami Muktananda still felt he was a long way from achieving their state of freedom. However, he never gave up. He was sure that sometime, somewhere, he would find that friend of God who would show him how it was done. Every time he heard about another great being, he would go to see him. And all the while, he did his best to honor everyone and everything as a form of God. He repeated the mantra, honoring himself as God. He never put himself down. One time, when he went to a holy river to bathe, he was approached by a priest who pestered him for two rupees for garlands. Muktananda was quite happy to buy a garland and perform the ritual, until the priest told him what it was. He was to repeat the mantra "I am a sinner. I was born in sin."

"No way," said Muktananda. "You can repeat that if you like, but I am not a sinner. I am perfect. I am the Self."

He said it, and he believed it, but at the same time, he knew he hadn't really understood it. He didn't know he was God the way he knew that candy was sweet. He hadn't merged with the mantra the way Athani Shiva Yogi had. And this was the state he longed for more than anything else in the world.

What more did he have to do? When he asked the great beings whom he met on his travels, they all said the same thing. "The Guru is the means," they said. "Go to a Guru. Worship the Guru. Stay with the Guru. Serve the Guru." And the scriptures said the same. Although Swami Muktananda loved and admired all the saints he met on his travels, he was still not ready to ask any of them to be his Guru. Years later he explained this by saying it was because he had so much pride in his learning. He thought he was different — that he would be able to do it on his own. Besides, he wasn't ready to settle down. He loved his pilgrimages. He loved striding barefoot along the roads of India from shrine to shrine. He loved the freedom and the solitude. There was nothing quite like setting off on a journey before dawn with only the mantra for company.

Yeola Baba

In India the rainy season, which lasts from mid-June to October, is called the monsoon. It follows the hot season, when the landscape turns dry and brown. The moment the heavy rains fall, the countryside turns green overnight. Rivers swell, and roads turn to mud. And at this season of the year, which is known as *chaturmāsa*, the Indian scriptures say that *sādhu*s should not go on pilgrimages. Instead they should stay in one place and meditate quietly. So Swami Muktananda would spend at least some months of each year in one place.

One of the regions he found himself drawn back to again and again was the state of Maharashtra. Maharashtra has been the home of hundreds of saints through the centuries, and some of them, in particular the ones who wrote devotional poetry and songs, are very famous—people like Eknath, Tukaram, Namdev, and Jnaneshwar Maharaj. Muktananda loved singing songs to God. He learned the songs of these saints, and later he sang and translated them for people all over the world.

In the town of Yeola in Maharashtra there was a monastery called the Somgiri Math where wandering *sādhus* could find a bed for the night. A man called Abhaji lived in a house opposite the Math. He was a good man who used to offer food and sometimes money to the *sādhus*. One day he noticed a *sādhu* whom he had not seen before. He was about twenty-five years old and was wearing a green shawl. It was Swami Muktananda, on his very first visit to Yeola. He did not speak the language, so Abhaji gestured to him asking if he would like to eat. In reply the *sādhu* extended his open palms. When Abhaji brought food from his house, Swami Muktananda received it in his cupped hands. He always ate straight from his hands in those days.

Later, Abhaji invited Swami Muktananda to his home. To him, as to many other people, this swami seemed special. It was as if he had more light than any of the others. Clearly he had great faith, in God and in himself. Soon Swami Muktananda was returning regularly to Yeola, and whenever he was in town he would come to visit Abhaji, who kept a veranda room aside for his use. As the years went by, the swami learned to speak the language of Maharashtra, which is called Marathi. Sometimes he and Abhaji would stay up half the night discussing verses from the scriptures. Abhaji liked it when the swami came to visit, for it had a good effect on him. It seemed that as he gave food and shelter to this young man, which he did for many years, his own worries were taken away.

Soon other people had heard of his special guest and were coming to meet Swami Muktananda. His presence, his wisdom, his authority, his humor, and his love of chanting God's name attracted an ever-growing band of followers. Young men used to gather at Abhaji's house to chant verses from the *Bhagavad Gītā*

and the *Vishnu Sahasranāma*. In the evenings, smaller boys would come to sing devotional songs, or *bhājans*. They called the swami who stayed with Abhaji "Baba," which means father and is a sign of love and respect. Every evening they would sit in a row on one side of their Baba, who always had a switch by his side in case anyone misbehaved. The older boys and grown-ups sat in a row on the other side. The little boys took turns to bring *seera,* sweet pudding, as *prasād* for everyone. One year, when the boys and young men numbered up to fifty, their Babaji led them in procession chanting *Hare Rāma Hare Krishna* all around the outside of the town. Swami Muktananda had become a local figure. Although, within himself, he still felt separate from God, his followers could see greatness in him. To them, he had become Yeola Baba.

One of those young men of Yeola was Babu Rao, who later became Swami Muktananda's personal attendant. He was a weaver by trade, but he loved to sing *bhajans*, and Baba encouraged him to play the harmonium even when others laughed at his efforts.

"Go on trying. You will learn. Everyone will sing after you," he told Babu Rao. Later Babu Rao would play the harmonium and sing *bhajans* to Baba with great love.

In those days they had only a small harmonium, and it didn't play well. Then one night, when Swami Muktananda had left town for a few weeks as he often did, Babu Rao was woken up by someone pounding on his door. He was scared out of his wits. Then, to his relief, he heard his Baba's voice.

"Babu, Babu, come open up your door. I've brought you great things. Come and see."

Babu Rao opened the door, and there stood Muktananda Baba with a huge tamboura in his hand. Beside him was an equally huge trunk.

"Open it!" he said to Babu Rao. "See what's in the trunk!"

"Babaji, it's one o'clock in the morning," said Babu Rao.

"Open it up!" Baba insisted. "Take it out and play it."

So Babu Rao opened the trunk. There, inside, was a fine, new, big harmonium with a beautiful tone. Baba had just brought it back from Bombay on the night train. He was ecstatic, because he had been chanting all the way home. God had sent a harmonium player and a *bhajan* singer as his fellow passengers on the train!

Then there was the time in Yeola when Baba recited the entire text of the *Jnaneshwari*. It took him a whole year to do it, because it is a very long book. It was written by Saint Jnaneshwar, who lived in Maharashtra in the thirteenth century, while he was still in his teens. It is a commentary written in the local language of Marathi on the ancient Sanskrit text called the *Bhagavad Gītā*. Jnaneshwar wrote it because ordinary people could not speak Sanskrit, and he wanted them to understand the great spiritual teachings contained in this conversation between Lord Krishna and the warrior Arjuna on the eve of a great battle.

Now, for the same reason, so that the ordinary people of twentieth-century Yeola could hear these teachings, Swami Muktananda recited a portion of the *Jnāneshwarī* every day of the year. Then, when the recitations were over, he held a weeklong chant of *Hare Rāma Hare Krishna* to honor Lord Krishna. The chant, or *saptah,* was attended by the local brahmin priest. As he chanted, this priest saw the child-god Krishna dancing among the circle of singers and musicians. He could hardly believe his eyes, and afterward he went to investigate the dust of the dancing circle. There, for him and everyone else to see, were the footprints of a tiny child.

At the end of that very same *saptah,* a huge feast, or *bhāndāra*, was offered. This was during World War II, and the government had restricted the amount of food that people could buy, in order to make it last. Rationing was not in the spirit of the Indian *bhāndāra*, however, and people brought large quantities of grain and sugar, lentils, oil, and ghee. All night long, Swami Muktananda moved quickly in the dark among the cooks, taking charge and supervising what they were doing. As the hour for the feast drew near, he noticed that people seemed nervous and uneasy. He asked what was wrong.

"What if the officials come and see all this food, Swamiji? They'll want to know where we got it. We'll be in terrible trouble.

They may even throw us in prison."

"If that happens," said Baba, "you just tell them Swami Muktananda did it all."

The hour came for the *bhāndāra*. Word had gone around all the villages, and soon people were seated in rows in the streets of Yeola. They all sang a hymn to Annapurna, the goddess of nourishment, and then Swami Muktananda's helpers moved down the lines serving everyone.

Above them, on a balcony overlooking the street, the government administrators watched. Swami Muktananda saw them, but took no notice. He just carried on fearlessly with the celebration. In the end the administrators went away and left them all in peace.

Another time during the war Swami Muktananda held a *saptah* to bring peace to the world. Throughout that *saptah,* he kept a lamp burning day and night in a blue glass dish in his veranda room in Abhaji's house on Bhoiwalla Street. In that room there was no chatter. People chanted *Om Namah Shivāya* all day, and in the evening they ended with a beautiful hymn. They sang it so slowly, with such feeling, that people stopped in the street below to listen.

The Haunted House

Swami Muktananda also stayed in other places in Maharashtra. For many years he spent part of the year in Chalisgaon. Because so many people followed him now wherever he went, it was necessary to find a large house to accommodate everyone. There was such a house in Chalisgaon village. It had three stories and it was empty. In fact, it had been abandoned. No one had dared to live in it for eighty years. And for one very good reason. It was haunted!

"That's fine, I'll live there," said Baba. "Ghosts don't bother me."

"No, but you don't understand, Baba," people told him. "These are terrible ghosts. Bad things happen to people who live there. They get ill. They have accidents. Please, Baba, please live anywhere else, but don't live there."

"Why should I feel scared of disembodied things?" said Baba. "My life is pure. I chant the divine Name. Don't you understand that ghosts can exist only in impure places? Ghosts flee when you chant the divine Name with all your heart."

And despite everyone's protests, he moved into the house.

Local people shook their heads. No good was going to come of this. The women of the village still brought him food, but they wouldn't come into the house with it. They went as near as they dared and then left it a few feet from the door. Entering the house became a test of faith. How far into the house dared they go? The ground floor? The next? The top floor? People who came from

Bombay to stay with Baba reported strange noises in the night. They would sense a disturbing presence. Sometimes they felt something trying to snatch their bedding away from them. Throughout all these alarms, Swami Muktananda was unmoved. The ghost was only a bundle of unfulfilled desires, he told people. It had lost its human form; it had lost its sense organs. And one day it would get tired and go away. And that is exactly what happened. In time the noises stopped. People no longer sensed an alien presence. The ghost had been released. It had gone away and left the house to Baba.

Kasara was another village near Yeola where Swami Muktananda lived from time to time. One day, in the late afternoon as the heat was going from the day, Baba was sitting outside the house with some of his followers, when a half-naked pauper passed through the village. As the man drew abreast of them, Swami Muktananda called him over. He gave him his mattress, his blanket, his shawl, and everything he was wearing except his loincloth. His followers felt anxious for him, for now he was half-naked. He would have to sleep on a wooden bed with no mattress. He would be cold without his blanket and his shawl.

Baba himself was unconcerned. He seemed happy and at ease. And at seven that evening, after the sun had gone down, before it began to get cold, a gentleman arrived from Bombay for Swami Muktananda's *darshan*. He knelt and placed at Baba's feet a blanket, a shawl, *dhotis,* and a carpet. One of the brahmin priests who had been present throughout said that at that moment, he understood that the supreme Lord was looking after Swami Muktananda.

Hanuman and the Hut at Suki

One day in Yeola, a man came to see Swami Muktananda because he was very worried about his wife. A few days earlier she had gone to draw water from the well on their farm. As she lowered the bucket into the well she had seen a vision of Hanuman, the monkey god who was servant to Lord Rama. Since then she kept falling into states of deep unconsciousness. Baba agreed to go and see the place, and the man hired a *tonga,* a light, horse-drawn carriage, and drove Baba to his farm.

It lay in a very beautiful landscape, surrounded by jungle, with mountains beyond. There, on the farmland near the well, were three small shrines under the mango trees. One of them was a shrine to Hanuman. As Baba stood there, he knew this to be a *tapovan,* a place where great spiritual practices had been performed in the past. He became more and more meditative as he walked back and forth across the land. The man's wife, meanwhile, had regained consciousness. Finally Baba returned to one particular spot.

"This is a good place for meditation," he said to the man. The man immediately invited Baba to stay there, and before sunset that day, the leaves had been cleared, and a hut was built out of sugarcane leaves and branches.

There are pictures of that hut and of the stone building that was later built in the shade of two mango trees. From his hut Baba could look out across the fields of sugarcane to the distant mountains. Baba loved mangoes, and when the fruit was ripe he always had something to eat. He hung a rope swing from one of the mango trees, and sometimes, when he had finished meditating, he would sit on the swing and rock back and forth, thinking about his meditation experiences. As always, people wanted to be with him. They would come to visit and have *satsang*.

At other times Baba would leave his hut and wander the hills

and fields, singing the songs of the poet-saints to the open sky. He would go to visit the shrines where their bodies were buried and sit for meditation where he could feel their energy still permeating the place. Or he would hear of a present-day saint and set off on a pilgrimage to meet him or her. For what he still longed for more than anything else in the world was to be in their state of consciousness. He wanted to know he was God the way he knew candy was sweet.

One of the saints Baba met in Maharashtra was named Hari Giri Baba. Hari Giri Baba was a character. He wore all his clothes at once, and very fine ones they were too—silk coats, one on top of the other, silk turbans, fancy shoes, and big baggy trousers. He roamed around, day and night, and spent a lot of his time walking along the dry bed of a river, picking up small stones. These he would admire and put in one of his many pockets. Sometimes he would gaze into the distance and scold. At other times he would talk to the wind.

One day, as Baba Muktananda watched him becoming more and more weighed down with stones, he asked him why he did it.

"What's so special if I collect stones?" replied Hari Giri Baba. "Other people, too, collect things. Coins. Paper. Jewels. Gold. Silver. Books. They too weigh themselves down. So what's the difference?"

The difference was that Hari Giri Baba's stones carried his spiritual energy, his *shakti*. When he gave them to people, those who knew how to listen could hear his laughter in them. They were gifts that brought great blessings.

Hari Giri Baba called Muktananda "Maharaj," which means "Great King." Baba could not understand this. He was a *sannyāsi*, not a king. Then one day Hari Giri Baba told him to visit an old fort. When Baba saw the deserted ruins, weeds sprouting from their broken battlements, he felt inconsolably sad. He went back to ask Hari Giri why he should feel this way.

"You were once king of that fort," Hari Giri told him. "In another lifetime you were a great and just ruler, and there you had happy times."

It was another lesson for Baba that everything we love and hold dear will one day turn to dust, and that we will not even remember it. It was also a sign that Hari Giri Baba knew things that were hidden to other people. So when Hari Giri made a prophecy one day, Baba listened, even though he did not know how true the saint's words would turn out to be.

"Soon you will no longer be just a *sannyāsi,* but a maharaj," said Hari Giri Baba. "You will no longer ask for anything. You will give to all."

It was while he was living at Chalisgaon that Swami Muktananda first heard about another great saint of Maharashtra, who lived in dilapidated houses and huts around the village of Nasirabad and was adored by Hindus and Muslims alike. His name was Zipru, but everyone called him "Anna," which means "elder brother" and is a sign of great respect. Swami Muktananda sent a man called Dadu and his friend to find out more about Zipruanna.

The men arrived in the village with offerings of coconuts, bananas, and sweets for Zipruanna. They asked where the saint could be found, and following the directions they were given, they found themselves in a back alley. The only person in sight was an old man—skinny, toothless, and stark naked—seated on a heap of garbage and smearing himself with filth. Around him some ten stray dogs rooted for food and scratched their fleas.

The men took one look and decided that if this was Zipruanna, the people who said he was a saint were wrong. This was no saint, this man was just plain crazy. They were about to beat a quick retreat, when Zipruanna spoke to them.

"Where do you think you're going? That's my fruit you have there. You were supposed to give it to me."

The two men looked at each other. How did Zipruanna know? Then, as they approached him cautiously to give him the fruit, he spoke to Dadu and said something even more remarkable.

"There is a photo frame in your house that contains the pictures of two *sannyāsis*."

"Yes?" said Dadu. For it was true, he did have such a frame.

"One of the *sannyāsis* is alive."

"Yes!" This was also true. And the living swami was none other than Swami Muktananda.

"Tell him he should come and see me."

Dadu did as he was asked. As soon as Baba heard Dadu's story, he set out immediately to meet Zipruanna.

The moment Baba saw him he knew that Zipruanna was not crazy, but in an exalted state. He had become one with God. This was the state Baba wanted for himself more than anything in the world, and so he began to visit Zipruanna a lot. As usual, Baba asked the question why? Why did

Zipruanna live on a heap of garbage? Why did he smear himself with filth?

"Better garbage outside than garbage inside my mind," said Zipruanna. "Besides, Muktananda, think about it. Isn't this whole universe the body of God?"

"Yes, Lord Zipru."

"Well, then garbage is part of the body of God along with everything else," said Zipruanna.

Baba fell silent. He could see that Zipruanna lived in the state of the Self, where all judgments had fallen away. Not only that, Baba could see that Zipruanna's body had become so pure through his spiritual practice that no filth could touch him. Although he spent most of his time seated in the middle of a garbage heap, Zipruanna gave off the most wonderful fragrance.

Like Hari Giri Baba, Zipruanna was omniscient. He could see past and future. He loved Baba and knew how much he longed to be one with God. He could also see what Baba still had to learn. Although Baba repeated the mantra, honoring the Lord within, he still acted as if God was elsewhere. He was still looking for Him in shrines and temples and other people.

"You are wasting your time wandering all over the country like this," he told him. "O you crazy one, God is within! Why do you seek Him outside?"

"Instruct me," said Baba.

"That is not for me to do," said Zipruanna. "Go to Nityananda in Ganeshpuri. Your treasure lies there. Go and claim it."

Nityananda! The very *sādhu* who had come to visit his school when he was a boy; the *sādhu* who had beckoned him from the crowd and stroked his face with his big gentle hands so many years ago; the *sādhu* he had visited on his pilgrimages over the years. Could it really be that this same Nityananda was the Guru that he had longed for? That all the dusty miles, the hungry days, the freezing nights, the many books he had read, the hard spiritual disciplines he had imposed upon himself had just been to make him ready?

The moment he heard Zipruanna say the words, Baba knew that it was true, and that somewhere deep within himself he had always known it. He wasted no more time. He set off at once for Ganeshpuri.

When he reached the village, he found there were long lines of people waiting in the street to see the great Siddha. He joined the line and waited his turn to have *darshan*. When, at last, he entered the house, he saw Bhagawan Nityananda lying on his side, his eyes half-closed and serene, as if his gaze were on an inner experience so absorbing that his attention never wavered from it. Nityananda Baba's hair was grey now and his legs were stiff with arthritis, but the power of his presence seemed greater than ever. Then Baba knew for certain that his years of spiritual practice had all been a preparation. For it was not Nityananda's state that had changed, but Baba's own capacity to experience it. And now, as he drew close, he understood something else as well. The question was not whether Nityananda was his Guru. It was whether he was Nityananda's disciple. Humbly, he knelt on the floor and bowed his head to Bhagawan Nityananda.

Nityananda Baba opened his eyes and looked at Swami Muktananda.

"So. You have come," he said.

The Perfect Disciple

People who saw Baba with Bhagawan Nityananda said that he was the embodiment of perfect humility in his Guru's presence. He never spoke unless he was spoken to, and he listened carefully to any instructions Bhagawan gave him so that he would never need to tell him twice. And Bhagawan spoke of Swami Muktananda with great respect. He called him "the learned young swami from the South."

Baba was fulfilled now, and overjoyed. He was a disciple. So that he could be near his beloved Guru, he found a place to stay in the neighboring village of Vajreshwari, in a small shrine behind the Devi temple. This was the very same place where Bhagawan had lived when he first came to the area. There Baba spent long hours in meditation, but every day he would walk across the fields just to have the *darshan*—the sight—of his Guru.

It was his custom, before he came for Bhagawan Nityananda's *darshan*, to bathe in the hot springs on the edge of the village of Ganeshpuri. Then he would walk into the village and visit the Shiva temple next door to Bhagawan's ashram. One day, when he

arrived for *darshan,* Bhagawan Nityananda asked him what he had been doing.

"I've been doing *pūjā,*" he replied. *Pūjā* means making offerings in worship.

"Where did you do the *pūjā?*"

"In the temple."

"What did you do?"

"I poured water on the *shivalingam,*" said Swami Muktananda. A *lingam* is a rounded stone, representing Shiva as pure Consciousness. There are *shivalinga* in temples all over India.

"What about the *lingam* of light within you?" asked Bhagawan. "Have you poured water on that? Only one who doesn't understand worships God on the outside. One who understands worships God on the inside. From now on, you should worship God on the inside."

With this command, Bhagawan helped Baba to truly understand. In searching the external world for God, he had been looking in the wrong place. God was within. To know Him, he had simply to rest in his own stillness.

A good deal of the time Bhagawan seemed to take no notice of Baba at all. In fact he would give *prasād*—presents, or food that he had blessed—to everyone except Baba. Sometimes he went even further. He would call Baba, as if to give him *prasād,* and then when Baba came up to get it, he would say, "No, not you. I didn't mean you."

In doing this, Bhagawan was working on Baba's ego—all those parts of Baba's personality that were getting between him and God. Bhagawan knew that if Baba was to become one with God, then all his pride in his learning and independence had to go. He had to learn the meaning of surrender.

Baba found this very hard. He never ever blamed or criticized Bhagawan for treating him like this, but sometimes he would feel he had to go away for a while. He would go back to his hut at Suki, to meditate beneath the mango trees. But now he could not eat any of his favorite fruit, because, without explaining why, Bhagawan Nityananda had told him not to. Even though he was a long way from his Guru, Baba did as he was told. For twelve whole years he never ate so much as a bite of mango, until one day Bhagawan gave him a mango as *prasād*.

Although he sometimes found it difficult to be with Nityananda, Baba could never stay away for long. His love and devotion always drew him back to Ganeshpuri for the *darshan* of his Guru. Bhagawan seemed not to take any notice of him, yet Baba noticed every single detail about Bhagawan. He knew that he rose at three and went to bathe in the hot springs. He knew that he walked for two hours before dawn. He knew that he ate very little, and very punctually, and that he spoke few words. He knew that he loved children, and that they were the only people allowed to make a noise in his presence. He knew that he didn't like too many lights after dark, and that people would sit quietly around him in the shadowy room.

He knew these things because day after day, he would come and watch quietly from the back of the hall as Bhagawan lay on a blanket on his wooden bed. Around this bed were tins of biscuits and dishes of sweets for the children. Then there were two more beds, one loaded with fruit and the other with cloth for *prasād*. Baba stood gazing at this scene for hours at a time. He loved the dark beauty of Bhagawan's body, which seemed to have a sheen like black crystal. He gazed at his belly, made strong and firm and big by Bhagawan's yogic breath control. He looked at Bhagawan's fingers, long like tiger's claws, and noticed that he never clenched his hands. Bhagawan's right hand was often in *chin mudrā*, with the first finger and thumb touching. His left was open in the *abhaya mudrā*, which gives the blessing of fearlessness. His eyes were half-closed, and his head swayed in ecstasy. When he laughed it seemed to Baba as if he scattered light all around him. From time to time there would come from his throat a sound of deep contentment which sounded like "Hunh."

Sometimes Baba's own eyes would close, but he would still see Bhagawan in his mind's eye. Sometimes when he went home, Bhagawan would appear to him as he sat in meditation. Baba always enjoyed his meditation when this happened, and soon, when he sat to meditate, he would try deliberately to make it happen. He would bring to mind every single detail of Bhagawan's appearance. He would remember the way he moved, the way he breathed, the comforting sounds of contentment that came from his throat. Gradually, as he did this, his meditations became deeper. He noticed happiness, courage, and strength growing in him. He began to feel more and more as if he were full of light. Sometimes he felt he actually was Bhagawan, and then he would feel drunk with happiness.

Although Baba never told Bhagawan what he was doing, it seemed as if Bhagawan knew. One evening he said to Baba, "Meditation on the Guru gives you life. All knowledge is in meditation on the Guru." These words were like a mantra to Baba. He thought deeply about them.

One night he stayed in the meditation hall at Bhagawan's house meditating on Nityananda all night long. That night he started to feel as if Muktananda no longer existed. He had become Nityananda, and he felt blissfully happy. At three in the morning, Nityananda called him. It was the time of the night called *brahmamūhurta,* when he always went to bathe in the hot springs. That night he took Baba with him. When they went back to Bhagawan's house, Baba resumed his meditation on Bhagawan till daybreak. Later, at *darshan*, Baba went up last as usual. Nityananda raised his hand in blessing.

"That's right," he said. "That's real meditation."

Divine Initiation

August 15, 1947, was a very important day in the history of India. It was the day when India became an independent country once again and was no longer ruled by the British. It was also a very important day in the life of Swami Muktananda.

It was his custom to go for Bhagawan's *darshan* in the evening. Usually Bhagawan would indicate when he should leave, and he would make his way home for the night. However on the eve of Independence Day, Bhagawan gave no sign, so Swami Muktananda stayed at his Guru's house and spent a happy night meditating on his Guru.

When morning dawned, the atmosphere was very calm. Bhagawan was still in his meditation hall as the sun rose in the sky, but he had started to make the little humming sounds in his throat that usually meant his meditation was nearly over. When he appeared, he was wearing a white shawl as well as his loincloth, and a pair of wooden sandals on his feet. This was unusual, for Bhagawan Nityananda always went barefoot. He seemed pleased and smiled at Baba. He touched him, then wandered away. After a little while he came back and stood right in front of him, staring into his eyes. Baba stared back transfixed. Finally Bhagawan made his familiar, comforting "Hunh" sound. Hearing it, Baba partially regained his normal consciousness.

"Take these sandals, put them on," said Bhagawan.

Baba was amazed. The shoes of a great being are very sacred. They carry his power, and no one who understood this would dream of wearing them.

"Gurudev, you have worn these *pādukās*. How can I wear them?"

Bhagawan laughed.

"If you really want to give them to me," Baba said, "let me spread my shawl, and then please be so gracious as to put your feet on it and leave your sandals there."

Gurudev agreed. He lifted one foot at a time and placed the *pādukās* on the shawl. Then he looked directly into Baba's eyes once more. Much to his amazement, Baba could see a ray of light coming from Bhagawan's eyes and going straight into him. Not only could he see it, he could feel it. It was searing, red hot, and so bright that it dazzled his eyes. Every hair on Baba's body rose in awe. He kept on repeating "*Guru Om, Guru Om*," as he watched this ray of light changing color from gold to saffron to brilliant blue. It seemed as if he had lost all sense of himself. Then, as he heard Bhagawan making his contented "Hunh" sound, he came out of his trance, knelt, and bowed his head to the sandals.

"Gurudev, what divine fortune this has been for me," he whispered. "I have received the greatest of blessings. Please live in these sandals with all your fullness, and let me worship them even if I don't know the correct way."

Bhagawan nodded. Then he gathered up more presents for Muktananda. Bananas, incense, flowers, some *kumkum*—Bhagawan brought them and laid them all on the sandals. Then he sat down close to Baba and spoke to him.

"All mantras are one," he told him. "All mantras are *Om. Om Namah Shivāya Om* should be *Shivo'ham. Shiva, Shiva* should be *Shivo'ham.* It should be repeated inside. Inside is much better than outside."

Then Bhagawan disappeared into his room. Baba had still not been told to leave, and so he continued to stand there, repeating the mantra inside himself as Bhagawan had just said he should. In a few moments Bhagawan came out again with a beautiful blue shawl in his hands, which he placed lovingly on Baba's shoulders. Finally Bhagawan went to the kitchen and brought back some newly fried *bhajiyās*, which he wrapped in a cloth and laid on the sandals with all the other gifts. Only then did he give Baba the signal to leave.

As he set off for home that day, carrying Bhagawan's sandals on his head, Muktananda was filled with wonder and gratitude. He knew he had been given a very special initiation, but he didn't know what he had done to deserve it. Bhagawan had so many devotees, so many disciples who seemed very close to him. Why had he chosen Muktananda as the one to receive his sandals? Slowly, savoring his good luck, he made his way toward Vajreshwari, singing *"Guru Om, Guru Om."*

A light breeze was blowing, and a soft rain began to fall. When Baba closed his eyes, he saw innumerable clusters of sparkling rays and millions of tiny twinkling sparks bursting within him. Those infinitely small sparks shimmered and coursed through his whole body at incredible speed. Baba looked with awe at their speed and number. Then he opened his eyes again and saw the same tender delicate blue sparks shimmering around him, mingling with the soft fine rain. He was moving so slowly that he did not know whether he was following the road or the road was following him.

As he reached the Gavdevi Temple, right by where Swami Muktananda's ashram Gurudev Siddha Peeth stands today, the thought "The Guru is inside, the Guru is outside" flashed into Baba's mind, and suddenly he knew, as surely as he knew that candy was sweet, that inside and outside were the same. They were One. He was one—with God and with the universe.

Tigers and Fields
of Burning Sugarcane

Several days later, when Swami Muktananda went for his Guru's *darshan*, Bhagawan told him he should go away for a while to his hut at Suki and meditate there. He gave Baba some fruit and sent him on his way. Baba was sad and a little worried to leave Bhagawan, but it never crossed his mind to disobey his Guru.

The hut between the mango trees was empty and waiting for him when he reached Suki. Baba put his Guru's sandals on his *pūjā,* or altar, and ate the fruit he had been given as *prasād.* Then he sat down to meditate. But now there was no more rapture, no more bliss. He was restless and agitated. He began to have visions of ugly, demonlike figures. He saw the whole earth spinning before his eyes. He saw the sugarcane field on fire. Then he heard the sounds of a camel and a tiger, and realized to his horror that there was no camel or tiger. These sounds were coming from him. The roaring of the tiger was so loud that the nearby villagers really thought there was a tiger in the sugarcane field. Baba knew he was in meditation, that none of this was real, but he was terrified all the same. He couldn't understand why it was happening. He forgot all about Vedanta, and being the Witness, and watching each thought and feeling as it came up. He forgot all about Kashmir Shaivism and seeing every thought and feeling as God. Instead, he thought he had done something terribly wrong. He thought Bhagawan Nityananda must be angry with him.

Just then, he saw a *tonga* coming across the fields toward him. It was his old friend Hari Giri Baba, grinning cheerfully as usual.

"O King, O Emperor, O Swami, get up, get up!" he shouted and burst into peals of laughter. "I know what is happening to you," he said, "but I will only tell you if you give me two rupees."

Baba gave him the two rupees.

"O Maharaj, good times have come for you, not bad. You are suffering from a beneficial fever. As a result of your fever, many people will be cured of their sickness and suffering."

Baba was comforted, but soon after Hari Giri Baba left, he was not so sure. His worries returned, and he decided to go away and live somewhere else, where no one knew him. So he took off his orange monk's robes and said goodbye to his hut, his swing, and his mango tree. Dressed in a white loincloth, carrying only his water bowl, he set off for the hills.

He reached Nagad, an isolated village in a beautiful landscape. There a rich landowner offered him a meal and a place to stay—another small hut where a yogi had been doing spiritual practices. The very first time Baba meditated in this hut, a voice came up inside him.

"Open that cupboard and read the book you find there," it said.

At first Baba took no notice. He was trying to meditate, and the voice was a distraction. But the voice kept on. In the end Baba gave up and opened his eyes. He looked around the room. Sure

enough, there was an old cupboard in the corner. Baba opened it. There was a single tattered book inside, full of secret teachings. It described exactly the sort of visions and feelings that had been coming to Baba in meditation. It called them *kriyās* and said they often happened when a seeker received *shaktipāt* initiation from his Guru. It said they were the result of the awakening of the spiritual energy known as *kundalinī*.

As he read this book, Baba understood that these things were coming up in him in order to be removed. He was being purified. All this was happening to make him greater and bring him closer to God. The visions were a gift from his Guru.

When he visited Zipruanna, the great saint confirmed this. Baba went to him one day with a very bad headache. In addition to all his other troubles, he was having a lot of headaches at this time. He told Zipruanna about his fearsome visions and Zipruanna nodded.

"A yogi on the path of the Siddhas should remember that

anything he sees in the light of the inner heart through the inspiration of the divine energy is the divine energy in its fullness. It may be good or bad, acceptable or repulsive, beautiful or ugly, beneficial or harmful, but it is all divine conscious energy."

And as Baba knelt to thank him, Zipruanna reached out and stroked his head.

"Your glory will reach the heavens," he told him. He pulled Baba into his lap and began licking his head the way a lioness might lick her cub. As he licked and stroked, Baba's headache began to ease. In fact, from that moment he was cured of his headaches forever. He returned to his hut in Nagad reassured, and resumed his meditation.

Realization

From then on, all Baba's anguish and confusion fell away. Although the terrible visions kept on coming, he didn't try to push them away, nor did he feel bad about himself for having such dreadful thoughts. Instead, he welcomed them as forms of God. As a result his *sādhana,* his spiritual progress, moved with the force of a river in flood. In meditation he saw visions of holy places, he heard inner sounds, he saw lights of different colors, including the beautiful blue light of the Self. His body discovered new postures, and soon he could sit in the full lotus posture for three hours without a break. His breath came in special ways, sometimes shallow, sometimes deep and slow. He saw valleys in the Himalayas that he had never visited and peaks he had never seen. He was taken to other worlds and other planets.

Throughout these experiences, which lasted for nine whole years, it seemed that Bhagawan always knew what was happening to him, even though he was a long way away. From time to time he would send people to Baba with messages that everything was going as it should. Once, when Baba was experiencing great heat in meditation, Bhagawan sent one of his devotees with a gift. It was a bottle of perfumed oil. Baba did not know why Bhagawan had sent it, but he rubbed a little oil on himself and a wonderful fragrance filled the air. The next day, Baba saw his Guru in meditation. Bhagawan handed him the same bottle of perfumed oil and said, "Your meditation will create more heat. It is the burning radiance of yoga. Use some scent every day."

The visions Baba had at this time were marvelous and extraordinary. Once a god, dressed in white silk with jeweled belt and sandals, drove him in a chariot at the speed of lightning to a fabulous city with beautiful trees, rippling streams, singing birds, and fearless animals. As Baba stepped down from the chariot, he realized that this beautiful place was Heaven, and that his charioteer had been none other than Indra, the king of Heaven himself.

Another time, he found himself transported to a place even more wonderful than Heaven. He traveled in a blue star. Though it looked small, it was large enough to contain him. The star carried him far away and set him down in a world too beautiful for words. Baba followed a small path and saw woods and caves and flowing streams of pure water. He saw white, blue, and green deer and white peacocks. The atmosphere was calm and peaceful and there was a wonderful blue light everywhere, such as you would see if you looked at the early morning sun through a piece of blue glass. So strong were the waves of *shakti* in Baba's body that he knew he was going to have the *darshan* of the ancient seers. He was right. He was in Siddhaloka, the world of those who have completed the spiritual journey and become Siddhas. As he moved through this place, he saw many Siddhas, all deeply absorbed in meditation. Some he recognized, others he did not. He saw Sai Baba of Shirdi and many

Siddhas from ancient times. He also saw Bhagawan Nityananda and understood that in addition to being alive on earth in Ganeshpuri, he also lived in Siddhaloka.

Baba spent a long time wandering around Siddhaloka, gazing at all the saints, yogis, and yoginis. No other world had seemed so good to him. He felt full of peace, happiness, and love. He did not want to leave. He sat down to meditate. As he did so, the blue star appeared, and, although he did not understand why, he felt compelled to go and sit in it. Immediately the star took him back at immense speed to his earthly place of meditation. As he arrived there, the star passed into the top of his head and exploded. Then a Siddha appeared, whom he did not know.

"You have just been to Siddhaloka," he told him. "In that place dwell the great saints who have achieved liberation. There one eats joy, drinks joy, lives in joy, and continually experiences joy.

No one can go there without the grace of a Siddha. Those who are following the Siddha path will attain full Siddhahood and will go to Siddhaloka. The blue star is the only way of traveling to it. And when the star explodes, the cycle of birth and death is broken, the bondage of karma is cut, and the veil of sins and good deeds is torn away." Then, having explained the importance of what had just happened to Baba—that the weight of his past actions, good and bad, had been lifted—he blessed Baba and disappeared.

The most wonderful light Baba saw in meditation was called the Blue Pearl. It was a brilliant point of blue light no bigger than a sesame seed. The first time he saw it, it shot out of his eyes with the speed of lightning, illuminating everything in every direction, and then went in again. Over time, as it appeared to Baba, its radiance increased, and as Baba became absorbed in it, love streamed through him. Then, as he neared the end of his long, courageous journey toward enlightenment, he had a vision in which the light of the Blue Pearl began to grow. It assumed the shape of an egg, and then that of a man. This was the Blue Person, the Lord Himself, Witness of all, shimmering and resplendent in His divinity. Baba had never seen anyone so beautiful. He marveled at His eyes, His hair, His long hands and slender fingers, His fine, soft clothes. He kept gazing at Him from head to toe, his eyes wide with amazement. Then the Blue Being spoke to Baba.

"I see everything from everywhere," He told him. "I see with My eyes. I see with My nose. I have eyes everywhere." He lifted up His foot a little and went on, "I see with this foot, too. I can see everywhere. I have ears everywhere. I can hear with every part of My body."

Later Baba was to see the Blue Pearl expand to become the shining, blazing, infinite Light of Consciousness. He saw the earth being born from this Light, just as surely as he could see smoke rising from a fire. Within the spreading blue rays, he saw his Guru,

Bhagawan Nityananda, his hand raised in blessing. When he looked again it was Lord Shiva with his trident who stood there. As Baba watched, Shiva changed as Nityananda had changed, and now he could see Muktananda—his body, his shawl, his *mālā* of *rudrāksha* beads—all made of blue light. Then there was Shiva again, then Nityananda, and then, as ice melts into water, Nityananda melted into Light, and there was nothing but shining Light with neither name nor form. And now the rays bursting forth from the Light contracted and became the Blue Pearl, which shrank back to the size of a sesame seed and merged into the space at the top of his head, the *sahasrāra*. At this point, Baba fell into a state of meditation beyond visions. When he came to, he saw all sorts of people, and in every single one was that same Blue Pearl he had seen in himself. Now he knew that the inner Self was real, and that it contained and had become everything and everyone. He knew it absolutely and forever. The state of being one with God was now his natural, permanent state. He was a fully realized being. He was a Siddha.

He was all alone in the big house in Chalisgaon that day, thirty-three years after he had set out from home and nine years after his *shaktipāt* initiation. But in Ganeshpuri, Bhagawan Nityananda, his Guru, who had guided him every step of the way, knew the very moment it happened. He sent one of his attendants out into the street to summon three of Baba's devotees who were waiting for *darshan*. They must come at once, said the attendant. Bhagawan wished to see them! The devotees followed the man into Bhagawan's house, where they saw him dancing jubilantly around the room.

"What are you doing here?" he cried. "Everything is there with him! Muktananda has become the supreme Lord! He is *Paramahamsa!* He is perfect! His name will become great throughout the world!"

Install Muktananda

The following year, rumors started to fly in Ganeshpuri that Bhagawan Nityananda was about to take *mahāsamādhi*, the great merging that happens when the body dies and the soul merges forever with God. Some of his devotees approached him and asked if the rumors were true. Bhagawan nodded affirmatively. His devotees became anxious and asked if they could build a temple in his honor. He indicated that a temple should be built behind the three rooms at Gavdevi. It would be a *samādhi* shrine, a temple where the body of a great being is buried.

After it was built Bhagawan sent for Swami Muktananda. When he arrived, Bhagawan Nityananda announced that he was not going to take *mahāsamādhi* just yet after all.

"But what about the shrine?" the people wanted to know.

"Install Muktananda," was Bhagawan's reply.

So Baba was installed in the temple next to the three rooms at Gavdevi, which Bhagawan had given to him to use when he came to visit. Now he told Baba to live there permanently. The temple became his home.

"He stopped my wandering," said Baba. "And with that, the wandering of many."

One of the first things Baba did when he settled in Ganeshpuri was to create a garden. Helped by a few devotees who came to see him on weekends, he cut bamboo sticks from the nearby woods, and during the week, when he was there alone, he trimmed them and bound them with hemp to make a fence. Then the ground was dug, and Baba went to nurseries in Bombay and brought back trees and plants which, by their beauty and fragrance, would create a calming, sacred atmosphere. When these were planted, Baba himself walked the half-mile to the river, back and forth, over and over again, to fetch water for them.

For as long as his own Guru was alive, Swami Muktananda remained a disciple. He wore white clothes, he lived simply, he went daily for his Guru's *darshan*, and he never spoke to anyone about his own great state.

Other people noticed there had been a great change in him, however. They found they were drawn into meditation in Baba's presence in exactly the same way as they were around Bhagawan. They noticed how much respect Bhagawan had for Baba. They noticed that he often sent seekers to Muktananda to have their questions answered. They compared notes and realized that the two great beings, a mile apart from each other, would often speak the same words at the same time. One day someone asked Baba about this.

"It seems I have an internal wireless station which picks up the signals from my Guru," Baba said, laughing.

Bhagawan Nityananda lived for five more years. Then in the summer of 1961 he became ill. One day in August he sent for Baba. When Baba came and knelt at his side, he stroked Baba's head.

"You will travel to distant countries," he told Baba. "The whole world will see you."

Then Bhagawan Nityananda put his hand deep inside Baba's mouth. He murmured secret mantras in his ear and gave him a final initiation, passing to Baba Muktananda the power of all the Siddhas. As this happened, Baba knew that Bhagawan Nityananda would soon leave his body. He became motionless. He and Bhagawan sat there for a long time, Bhagawan resting his hand on Baba's head. Then, at about eleven o'clock at night, he told Baba to go. Baba did as he was told. He sat outside Bhagawan's rooms for a while, getting used to the idea that Bhagawan was about to leave his body. Then he spent the rest of the night letting people know that Bhagawan was not feeling well, and if they wanted to see him, they should come soon.

Two days later, Bhagawan Nityananda took *mahāsamādhi*. Though he would live on in the hearts and minds of all his thousands of devotees, he had reached the end of his life in his physical body.

Baba was full of grief. Yet he took care of the funeral ceremonies and made sure that all the people who had come for their final *darshan* with Bhagawan were fed and looked after. When it was all over, he returned to his own small ashram and wept.

He wept because he had loved his Guru so much and because he would never see him again in his physical body. Yet he also knew that Nityananda could never leave him because he and Nityananda had become one—with each other, with God, and with everything and everyone in the universe. "It is his radiance in the light of my eyes," he said. "Through my breathing, it is he who comes in and goes out."

The Guru Years

Baba Muktananda spent the rest of his life in service to his Guru. Even though his ashram grew bigger, he himself still lived in the three simple rooms that Bhagawan had given him, surrounded by pictures of his Guru. He continued to chant and meditate, and every day he would go to the temple in Ganeshpuri village for the *darshan* of Bhagawan Nityananda's *murti*, or statue. Then he would return home and sit in the courtyard of his ashram as people came for his *darshan*.

Right from the start he insisted that everyone who stayed with him, young and old, follow the ashram discipline. They were asked to respect themselves and each other, and to remember that the ashram was a sacred place, a place where people could find themselves drawn into meditation. This meant talking only when necessary, and then very softly. It meant following the ashram schedule and playing a part in the everyday running of the ashram. Baba said that people who were absorbed in their work around the ashram—their *guruseva*—were in a state of natural meditation. Visitors noticed this too. They felt the quiet and stillness as soon as they stepped in from the street.

Baba participated in *guruseva* with his devotees. Many people remember seeing him tend his garden in the early days. Among them was a little girl, who had been brought to Bhagawan by her father when she was younger. Bhagawan had seemed to wave her away.

"For him, for him," he had said, meaning that her father should take her to Swami Muktananda's ashram.

Now that young girl came often and stayed with her parents in Swami Muktananda's ashram. Her name was Malti. She used to wake up at two-thirty in the morning just so that she could watch Baba watering the roses in the dark. This he would do very gently and lovingly, singing the mantra and caressing the blooms, which were always big and healthy.

The ashram had its own well by this time, and the water for the garden was brought to Baba in tin cans by the light of kerosene lamps. Baba transferred the tins of water to the watering can and used them faster than people could carry them. One day

several of his devotees who came up from Bombay on weekends grumbled secretly among themselves about this. They came to meditate, they said, and instead they had to work. What were they getting out of all this, they asked each other.

Later that same day one of them was in the kitchen when he came face to face with Baba. He said Baba looked like Rudra, the angry face of Shiva. And Baba began to shout at him.

"So! What are you getting out of coming to Baba?" he yelled. "Nothing! Right? That's what you think?"

The man trembled, wondering how Baba knew what he and his friends had been saying.

"I have a whole ocean to give!" Baba went on. "But do you have the capacity to hold it? No! That's why I make you do *seva*. It's to make you strong. Only after you serve the Guru are you able to take what the Guru can give. Only then can you hold it."

Baba was a magnetic being—dynamic, supple, full of vigor. He was everything by turns: compassionate as well as strict; learned and simple; funny and serious; down-to-earth and yet, at other times, almost ethereal. It seemed there was no skill that he had not mastered: cooks, musicians, gardeners, scholars, engineers, psychologists, physicians, and children all found they could learn from him.

For just as when he was a boy, he and his friends had loved to be with Bhagawan Nityananda, so now children were drawn to Baba. He was playful and full of stories. Once Malti told him that a ten-year-old girl had confided in her that she was unhappy because she never received any "fruit," or results, from her meditation. Baba told Malti to place two mangoes in front of the girl the next time she sat to meditate. When the ten-year-old opened her eyes she was very surprised, but when Malti told her how the mangoes came to be there, she loved the joke.

For all his playfulness, Baba always kept the goal of the ashram clearly before everyone. It was to help them all, young and old, understand that they were embodiments of the Self. In order to understand this, young people were expected to do *sādhana*, spiritual practice, like everyone else. They attended the chants, and during the chanting of the *Bhagavad Gītā*, Baba made sure they were seated at the front where he could keep an eye on them and help them to pronounce the Sanskrit words properly. He told them the stories he himself had loved as a child. And as he did these things, he was teaching even the youngest of his disciples the same way Bhagawan had taught him. He would play with their expectations, sometimes giving them *prasād*, sometimes not. In this way he helped them understand that it is expectations that cause suffering. He showed them that the Guru's *prasād* was not just for them personally, it was for everyone.

It wasn't only people who were deeply affected by knowing Baba Muktananda. Animals loved and obeyed him too. One time some ashram children spotted a baby cobra that had fallen into the well. For hours they tried to catch him in their buckets, without sucess. The cobra kept slithering away. Then Baba arrived and peered into the well.

"Come on, get into the bucket," he called to the cobra.

The cobra did not move.

"What's wrong? Don't you trust me?" said Baba. "Get into the bucket."

To the children's surprise, the cobra did exactly as he was told. They hauled him up and Baba set him free.

Then there was Vijayananda, the ashram elephant, who had been a present to Baba from a devotee. He was a fine animal, with all the marks that the scriptures describe as auspicious, but he was also temperamental. His trainers, or mahouts, were scared stiff of his temper, and he knew it. Baba, on the other hand, was not afraid of him. Once when he ran amok, Baba grabbed him by the trunk and held on until he calmed down. After that, all he ever had to do to calm Vijay was raise a warning finger.

Vijay used to come to the courtyard every day. There Baba would feed him sugarcane, mangoes, and chocolates. He would talk to Vijay, play with him, and give him oil baths. And Vijay would kneel to Baba, garland him, and lay his trunk on Baba's head.

Then one time, when Baba was away from the ashram, Vijay ran amok again. He escaped, trumpeting in fury, tearing up everything in his path. No one could do anything with him. Baba was in America at the time, but the ashram manager reached him on the telephone.

"Go out into the field and say to him, 'Baba says you should go back to the house,'" Baba told the manager.

So, rather nervously, the manager went out into the rice field and shouted to the elephant from a distance.

"Vijay! Baba says you should go home!"

The elephant didn't hesitate. Calmly, majestically, he made his way across the rice field into the ashram and back to his shed.

Over the years, more and more people came to meet Baba. Devotees brought friends, and friends brought friends, and soon new buildings had to be built to house and feed everyone. Baba knew that this expansion was only the beginning of the task his Guru wanted him to do. He would tell people sometimes, as they sat around him in the courtyard, that one day he would travel to distant countries to tell others about the joy of the inner Self. He would bring the teachings of the Siddhas, which became known as Siddha Yoga meditation, to seekers everywhere. And one day the ashram would become a center of learning and spiritual practice for people of all religions from all over the world.

This didn't seem very likely to many of his listeners. Of course they knew that Baba was a great being, but Ganeshpuri was in the middle of nowhere. There was still jungle around it, and local roads were bad. What foreigner would want to come and live there? But within a few years, the first foreigners started coming. They were happy to stay in the ashram, which was growing year by year, and they loved Baba. Baba spoke in Hindi or Marathi, so most of the Westerners could not understand what he was saying, but it didn't matter. They soon found themselves drawn into deep states of meditation just by being in his presence. They saw visions and heard mantras they didn't know coming from their own mouths. Their bodies went into spontaneous yogic postures. Above all, they were given the experience of boundless love—their own and Baba's. They were given the experience of the Self, and thereafter their lives were transformed.

The Meditation Revolution

A lmost as soon as Westerners started arriving in Ganeshpuri, they asked Baba to visit their countries. Baba didn't accept their invitations at first. He was waiting until the time was right and he received a message from his Guru. In 1970, that message came. Baba saw Bhagawan Nityananda in meditation. And Bhagawan revealed that the time had come for him to travel once again—this time to the West to transmit *shaktipāt* to thousands of people. And so began Swami Muktananda's Meditation Revolution. The changes he was going to bring were not social or political. They were changes within individual human beings, that came about when he awakened them to their own inner greatness.

He traveled to many countries—America, Australia, Europe—and everywhere people came to be with him. In the beginning, everything needed on tour had to be taken along. After each program, Baba's chair and the musical instruments and all the pots and pans for the kitchen had to be packed into vans and driven on to the next city. No matter how much there was to do, meditation always took place in the morning. The *Guru Gītā*, a Sanskrit chant that explains how a human being can become one with God, was sung every day. Meals were cooked under Baba's supervision. If people neglected to sing the evening *āratī* in praise of Bhagawan Nityananda, Baba Muktananda would round people up and tell them:

"It is Nityananda's *shakti* which upholds this tour." He would say, "You should never forget the evening *āratī*." And, "I am only here because I received the inner command from my Guru. I'm not here on my own."

As he traveled, more and more people came to see this Guru with the woolly hat and the dark glasses. Rich and poor, young and old, film stars, astronauts, politicians, housewives, and professors came to sit at his feet. Baba taught them to chant and to meditate. He told them about the great beings he had met, and he sang them the songs and prayers of the poet-saints, the songs and prayers he had sung as he walked alone beneath the Indian sky. Above all, he told them the stories he had loved since childhood.

One of his favorite stories, which he told with great verve and humor, came from a poem by the Marathi poet Ramachandra. It was about a man who sat down in the shade of a wish-fulfilling tree.

He was very happy to find himself beneath such a fine tree, but he thought life would be much improved if he had a house to live in. Immediately a beautiful bungalow appeared before him.

"This is all right," thought the man, and he went inside. "But it would be even better if I had something to eat. And some decent plates to eat from."

Quick as thought, all his favorite foods appeared before him on plates of burnished gold.

"Fantastic," thought the man. "Although I could do with a few servants to wait on me."

Immediately he was surrounded by servants, immaculately dressed in white coats with silk sashes and turbans. They served him course after course of delicious foods, until he could eat no more. Then the man waved them away and patted his belly contentedly.

"What a man in my position needs," he said to himself, "is a beautiful young wife."

Instantly there appeared before him a young woman of ravishing beauty. Never in his wildest dreams had he imagined such a lovely wife. For the first time, a doubt crossed his mind.

"Hang on," he said. "This is too good to be true. Beautiful women don't just appear out of thin air. What if she is a demon?"

The moment he thought it, that's what she became. And then the man thought, "I was right! My goodness—what if she eats me up?" And the moment he had that thought, that is exactly what happened. He disappeared along with the woman, the servants, the food, the plates, and the house. His mind had destroyed his world as surely as it had created it.

Despite all the crowds around him, Baba Muktananda was not interested in becoming famous or in gathering disciples for himself. What was most important to him was giving *shaktipāt*, the spiritual awakening that would begin the process of removing everything that prevented people from experiencing themselves as God. Most of those who came to meet him hadn't searched as hard or as bravely as he. They had little or no idea what it meant to become one with God or to have a Guru, but Baba made *shaktipāt* initiation available to all. He even created special programs known as Intensives to enable him to give *shaktipāt* to first hundreds and then thousands of people at the same time. And in case, like him, they had experiences that frightened them, he wrote a book called *Play of Consciousness,* all about his own *sādhana,* so that they could read it and understand what was happening. He wanted them to know that everything that came to them in meditation was a form of God and that there was nothing to be afraid of.

"A lion is roaming the world," said one spiritual leader who met Baba on one of these tours. "And wherever he goes, he frees people to love God, to have faith in their own divinity."

It was true. Baba Muktananda told people over and over again: "Meditate on your own Self; honor your own Self; kneel to your own Self; worship your own Self; your God dwells within you as you."

In his presence people experienced the truth of what he was saying, and that experience transformed them. Just meeting Baba made them want to give up their bad habits. Many people understood that they had been looking in the wrong place for happiness and contentment. They came up in the *darshan* line and every night, among the gifts, were substances people longed to be free from—cigarettes, alcohol, and other drugs.

"This will take you much higher," Baba said to one young boy who had given him a packet of marijuana. And he handed him a mantra card with the mantra *Om Namah Shivāya* on it. The marijuana was put in a display cabinet with all the other drugs, alcohol, and cigarettes people had given him. He kept them in the cabinet so that other people might see them and be inspired to give up their addictions.

Another time a young man came up in the *darshan* line, and Baba asked him what he did for a living.

"Nothing," said the young man, with a happy smile. "Somehow, ever since I've been on the spiritual path, God has been taking care of me."

"Have some mercy on God and get a job," Baba said.

No matter how busy he was, or how many people came to see him, Baba always gave each one what was needed. Once, in the middle of a long *darshan* line, a little boy came up with a fingerprinting set and asked Baba if he could take his fingerprints.

"What do I have to do?" asked Baba.

The boy showed him. So Baba had all his prints taken, one by one, while the line waited. His hands were covered with ink, but he didn't care. He was completely absorbed in the game of fingerprinting. Then, when the boy had gone off happily with a full set of his prints, Baba gave his attention to all the other people in the *darshan* line.

As a result of Baba's three world tours, Siddha Yoga Meditation Ashrams and Centers grew up all over the world. In Oakland, California, and South Fallsburg, New York, hotels were bought and renovated and turned into beautiful ashrams. Baba was interviewed on television and radio. He gave talks in places like Carnegie Hall in New York City and in a huge tent by the Pacific Ocean in Santa Monica, California. A Jewish organization gave him an award named after a great Jewish mystic. He was invited to attend the opening of the Black National Theatre in Harlem. There a woman asked him what she could do about her negative feelings toward white people.

"You should remember that people are neither black nor

white, but blue," said Baba. He was talking about the Blue Being: the Self, the Knower that lives in every human heart. He was demonstrating that a great being sees through outer appearances to the great Truth within.

Baba could see this greatness in everyone, even when other people couldn't. One summer a young French boy called Jean came to stay in the ashram. He had a stutter, and this made him frustrated, so that often he was angry and aggressive. At one stage his behavior was so bad that the adults taking care of the Children's House thought they were going to have to ask him to leave. Then one day, during *darshan*, he stood up front watching Baba intently for a long time. People who knew him were wondering if he was up to something—but Baba didn't seem to mind, and he was allowed to stay as long as he wanted, undisturbed. Finally he went for Baba's *darshan*, and Baba gave him the spiritual name Siddhartha. Jean wanted to know what the name meant. He was very proud when he was told that Siddhartha was the name by which the Buddha was known when he was young, and from then on he insisted that everyone call him Siddhartha.

Now it so happened that just a few days earlier Baba had been saying in an evening program how much he had been inspired by the stories of Prahlad and Dhruva. He told how he and his friends had acted out the stories of the saints. The devotees running the Children's House had an idea. They would put on a play about the young Buddha in French, and Jean would star as the Buddha. They told him, "Jean, if you're going to play the Buddha, you'll have to start acting like the Buddha." They made a big chart for him. At the bottom it said, *Je m'appelle Jean,* "My name is Jean," and at the top, *Je m'appelle Buddha,* "My name is Buddha." Every day that he acted like the Buddha, he would move higher up the chart. As he rehearsed the play and learned his lines, it was clear that Jean was learning new ways of being. He was especially taken by the scene where a man shouted every sort of insult at the Buddha, and the Buddha refused to retaliate. When the man grew tired of shouting and fell silent, the Buddha asked, "If you invited guests to your house, and they did not eat the food you offered, what would you do?"

The man replied, "Why, eat it myself, of course."

"I have not eaten all the abuse you hurled at me," said the Buddha. "Now you will have to eat it. That is the way it is with anger. In the end it hurts you more than it hurts me."

Finally the great day arrived when the play was to be performed. "Today I really am the Buddha," said Jean, his eyes shining with excitement. As the play unfolded he gave a great performance. He didn't make a single mistake. He didn't stutter once. At the end came the powerful moment when the Buddha reaches enlightenment beneath the bodhi tree. Jean sat in full lotus position. The audience was completely silent. Then Jean opened his eyes, winked, and waved. The next day he went back to France with his chart under his arm and a picture of Baba pointing at him as if to remind him who he really was.

More and more children came with their parents to see Baba. He decided that the time had come to give Siddha Yoga Meditation Intensives especially for children. Often led by devotees who were still in their teens, these Intensives were for young people between the ages of six and sixteen. They weren't as long as the Intensives for adults, but the children had many of the same inner experiences as their parents did. This is what Baba told the young people at the end of one of the first Intensives:

"You should all go to school without fail. You should not be too naughty, but you can play. You should not learn bad habits in school.

"Once upon a time I was young just like you. Look at me now! You should know that, although you are still young, goodness lies within you. You should always think well of yourself. You should meditate every day. You should also chant a bit. When you are in school, when you are with your friends, you can talk about meditation. You can talk about Siddha Yoga."

Baba's words inspired many children and young people to be better students at school. Their minds were clearer and more focused as a result of meditation. They felt good about themselves because they knew they were growing toward Baba's state. Baba helped them to strengthen their memory and concentration in other ways too. There is a Sanskrit chant of great complexity called the *Rudram.* At one time Baba had the teenagers in the ashram learn this chant. When scholars came to visit they were amazed at the way in which young people from different countries chanted together with perfect pronunciation, many of them from memory. When the children returned home their teachers were also impressed. They did not know about meditation or the *Rudram,* but they certainly saw a change in their students. Their classwork improved and they did well on their exams. They behaved responsibly, treating their teachers and classmates with love and respect.

Such were the changes that Baba brought about with his Meditation Revolution.

The End of a Perfect Life

Through his last years, as he traveled the world writing books, teaching, and bestowing *shaktipāt*, Baba was tireless. And all the time, knowing his physical body was mortal, he was preparing someone to take over his Guru's work when he was no longer able to do it.

Just as Bhagawan had known Baba from the time he was a boy, so Baba had known the person he chose as his successor from the time she was a small girl. She had been the child of whom Bhagawan had said, "For him, for him"; the girl who had woken up especially early so she could watch Baba watering his roses; the girl called Malti, now grown up. She loved Baba more than anyone in the world, and she worked hard in his service. From her earliest years, Baba had supervised her meditation practice and watched over her *sādhana*. It seemed that he knew her future from the start. One day, when she was quite young and her family was being photographed with Baba, she ran away and hid.

"Maybe she knows she will always be with me, so she doesn't see the need for photographs," said Baba.

As Malti grew older, she became Baba's interpreter, translating for him on his world tours. In time she took the vows of *sannyāsa*, as Baba himself had done, and was given the name Swami Chidvilasananda, which means the "bliss of the play of Consciousness." Not long afterward, Baba passed on to her the power of all the Siddhas just as his Guru had passed it on to him. Then he announced that he was going into retirement, and henceforth devotees should regard Swami Chidvilasananda as his successor, the living Guru of the Siddha lineage.

Later that same year, on the night of the full moon early in October, Baba Muktananda took *mahāsamādhi*. His full and perfect life had come to a peaceful end. The boy who longed to know God had achieved his ambition. The boy had become a *sādhu*, the *sādhu* had become a saint, and finally the saint had become a great, great Guru. Now it was time for his spirit to shed the body in which he had achieved so much and merge forever and completely with God, the Absolute.

For his followers, it was a time of deep sorrow. Never again would they see Baba in his physical form. Yet, to their astonishment, along with their grief many people experienced the bliss, love, and expansion they felt when Baba was alive. They came to understand that what the sages said was true: when a great being dies, his divine *shakti* spreads across the universe like the rays of a great light.

This state of eternal light and bliss was what Baba had always wanted for others. He wanted everyone to know it was always there within them, no matter what happened to them on the outside. He wanted them to live in that state all the time, as he had done—the state of Zipruanna and Hari Giri Baba, of Siddharudha Swami, Athani Shiva Yogi, and his own beloved Guru, Bhagawan Nityananda. Exactly one week before his death, in the last television interview he gave, in the Himalaya Mountains in Kashmir, he spoke of his great wish for mankind.

Baba said, "I want to see this world full of saints. I want to see everyone happy. Everyone should live in constant bliss and should not even dream of unhappiness. This is my last wish to God. And finally, I am going to give you this divine message:

> Meditate on your own Self;
> Worship your own Self;
> Honor your own Self;
> Bow to your own Self;
> Your God dwells within you as you."

Epilogue

If you go to Gurudev Siddha Peeth in Ganeshpuri, India, you will find the Samadhi Shrine of Swami Muktananda Paramahamsa. This is the temple where his body is buried—the very same temple that Bhagawan had built, and where he told his devotees to install Muktananda. It is made of white marble, and in that still and beautiful place you can experience for yourself that even after a great being leaves his physical body, his energy, his *shakti,* lives on.

We can experience Baba's *shakti* in other ways, too. It is in every Siddha Yoga Meditation Ashram and Center throughout the world. It is there in every program, in every chant, and in every practice we do at home. It is in the many beautiful books he wrote. It is there whenever we follow Baba's command and remember to honor ourselves and one another as God.

Above all, Baba's *shakti* is there in the living Guru, his successor Swami Chidvilasananda, affectionately called Gurumayi, who today carries on Baba's work. Completely immersed in that same ecstatic state, she bestows *shaktipāt* initiation on seekers of all ages. Like Baba, her only wish is that as many people as possible discover the bliss of the inner Self.

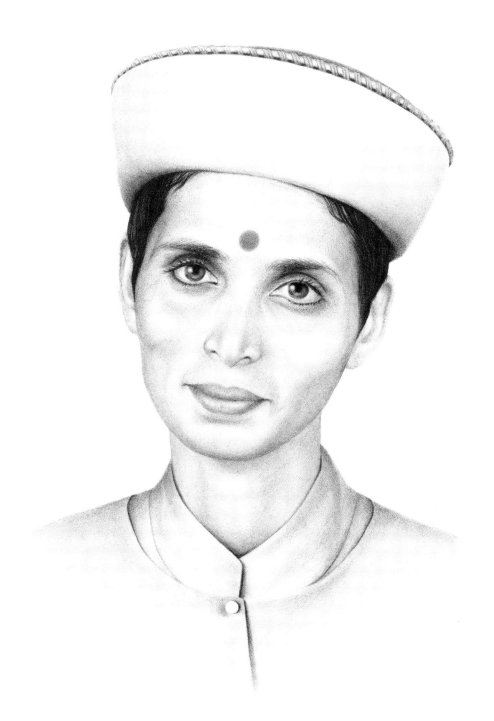

Pronunciation Guide for Sanskrit Words

Next to the less familiar Sanskrit (and some Hindi) words in the glossary there is a guide, in brackets, to help you pronounce the word. In Sanskrit, a vowel can sound one of two ways, depending on whether it is short or long. These sounds are given in the key below. Short vowels look just like vowels in English (a, i, u). Long vowels in the text have a bar over them, and in the pronunciation guide, they are shown as double vowels (aa, ee, oo, ay) or as the letter o. In Sanskrit pronunciation, the long vowel sound is held for twice as long as the short vowel sound. This often gives the effect of accenting, or stressing, the syllable in which a long vowel appears. In the glossary pronunciation guide the vowels of any accented syllables are written in capital letters.

Key

a as in *a*bout   *u* as in f*u*ll
aa as in f*a*ther   *oo* as in sch*oo*l
i as in p*i*t   *ay* as in pl*ay*
ee as in f*ee*t   *o* as in h*o*me

Glossary

abhaya mudrā [a bhAya mu drAA]: (*abhaya* means "fearlessness," *mudrā* means "a lock or seal") a gesture made by raising one hand with the palm facing outward, meaning "do not fear." *Mudrās* are hand gestures that seal in energy. Saints are often pictured making these gestures as a way of giving their blessings.

Absolute: the highest Truth; God.

āratī [AA ratee]: a ceremony in which lights, incense, and other objects are waved before a saint or image of God while chanting a hymn. Also, the hymn chanted during this ceremony.

ashram [AA shram]: ("without worldly fatigue") a place where spiritual practices such as meditation, chanting, and offering service are performed; also the home of a Guru or saint.

Bhagavad Gītā [bhAga vad gEEtaa]: ("song of the Lord") one of the major Indian scriptures, part of the epic known as the *Mahābhārata*. In this dialogue, Lord Krishna explains to his disciple, the warrior Arjuna, the way to know the Self. The discussion takes place on a battlefield where two royal families are at war.

Bhagawan [bhAga wan]: one who is divine. A title of the greatest honor, which means "the Lord."

bhājan(s) [bhAA jan]: songs sung in devotion to God.

bhajiyā(s) [bha jiyAA]: a vegetable or fruit dipped in a batter of flour, water, and spices and then deep fried.

Blue Pearl: a brilliant blue light, the size of a tiny seed (also known as the *bindi*, or point), which can be seen in meditation; the inner Self resides there. The Blue Pearl is the means by which the soul travels to the different worlds, either in meditation or at the time of death.

bodhi tree: pipal, or sacred fig tree of India; the tree under which it is believed the saint Gautama attained enlightenment and became the Buddha.

boon: a blessing, something that is asked or prayed for and received.

brahmamūhurta [brahma mOO hurta]: the early morning hours between 3:00 and 6:00. The Indian scriptures say this is the best time for meditation and prayer.

brahmin: a member of the priest caste in Indian society. They perform religious ceremonies.

Buddha: ("enlightened") the title of the Indian saint and philosopher Gautama.

caste: an inherited class or grouping of people in Indian society.

chakra(s) [cha kra]: ("wheel") a center of energy located in the subtle body in each person. There are seven major *chakras* in the body. Each *chakra* has different qualities that are purified by the *kundalinī* energy as it moves up through the body.

Chidvilasananda, Swami: the name given to Gurumayi by Baba Muktananda at the time she took the vows to become a monk. It means the "bliss of the play of Consciousness."

chin mudrā [chin mu drAA]: (*chin* means "Consciousness") a hand gesture made with the tip of the thumb and the index finger touching while the other three fingers are outstretched. It is practiced during meditation to keep the spiritual energy circulating throughout the body.

Consciousness: the highest awareness; the intelligent, alive, divine awareness that creates, supports, and pervades the entire universe.

dal: a spicy soup made from different types of lentils, a very good source of protein; also, the edible seed this soup is made from.

darshan [dAr shan]: seeing God or an image of God; seeing or being in the presence of a saint or a sacred place.

Devi [dAY vee]: the goddess; the female aspect of God.

Devi temple [dAY vee]: a shrine that honors the Devi, the female aspect of God.

dharma: one's duty in life; the path of righteousness, correct behavior. The highest *dharma* is to recognize the Truth in one's own heart.

dhoti [dho tee]: a piece of cotton cloth worn by men in India. It is tucked in at the abdomen and forms loose-fitting pant legs, ideal for hot and humid weather.

Ganges: the most sacred river of India, located in the North and named after the goddess Ganga. It is believed that all sins are washed away by entering this river.

ghat: a passage or stairway to a river. At certain rivers, funeral pyres are erected on the waterfront ghats, and the remains of the bodies are then put into the river.

Guru: (from "darkness" *gu*, to "light" *ru*) a spiritual teacher or master who has become one with God and who guides seekers to that same state of oneness.

Gurudev [gu ru dAYv]: another name for the Guru, a title of the highest respect and affection.

Gurudev Siddha Peeth: the name of the main ashram of Siddha Yoga, and the place where Baba Muktananda is buried. It is located in Ganeshpuri, India. A *siddha peeth* is a sacred "dwelling place of the Siddhas." This ashram was named by Baba Muktananda in honor of his beloved Gurudev Nityananda.

Guru Gītā [gu ru gEEtaa]: a Sanskrit chant entitled the "song of the Guru." It is a dialogue between Lord Shiva and his beloved goddess Parvati in which he explains the mystery of the Guru-disciple relationship. Baba Muktananda has said this is the "one indispensable text."

Gurumayi: a name of respect and endearment often used when addressing Swami Chidvilasananda.

Guru Om [gu ru Om]: the mantra by which the inner Self is remembered in the form of the Guru.

guruseva [gu ru sAYva]: work or service offered to the Guru for the sake of the Self, without expecting rewards or payments. It is one of the main practices of Siddha Yoga.

Hare Rāma, Hare Krishna [ha rAY rAA ma, ha rAY krish nA]: a chant praising Lord Rama and Lord Krishna.

harmonium: a small keyboard instrument, often played during chants.

hatha yoga: a branch of yoga that teaches physical and mental postures or exercises and breath control as a means of purifying and strengthening the body.

Hindu: a person who follows Hinduism, the major Indian religion as taught in the Vedic scriptures, the Upanishads, and the *Bhagavad Gītā*.

karma: ("action") any action—physical, verbal, or mental. Also, a person's destiny, which is caused by past actions. In order to reach the goal of Self-realization, one needs to be freed from the consequences of one's actions, or karma.

Krishna, Lord: an incarnation of Lord Vishnu, Lord Krishna lived during the time of the struggles between the warring royal cousins, the righteous Pandavas and the wicked Kauravas. His teachings are to be found in the *Bhagavad Gītā*, one of the main Indian scriptures.

kriyā(s) [kri yAA]: ("movements") any physical, mental, or emotional activity caused by the awakened *kundalinī* in order to purify the mind, body, and nervous system so the seeker can experience higher states of Self-awareness.

kumkum: red-colored powder made from the tumeric plant and used for putting an auspicious mark, or *bindi,* between the eyebrows in remembrance of God and the inner Self. Indian women also customarily wear this mark to signify they are married.

kundalinī [kunda li nEE]: ("coiled") the supreme cosmic power, or *shakti,* which exists coiled up at the base of the spine. Once the *kundalinī* energy is awakened through the Guru's grace, it travels upward through the subtle channel near the spine to the crown of the head. There it merges with the universal Self and the seeker attains oneness with God. The Guru awakens and guides this energy to its final destination.

lotus posture: a sitting position in hatha yoga where both legs are crossed over each other with the feet resting on the thighs. This is a good posture for meditation.

lungi [lun gee]: a long piece of cotton material worn by Indian men wrapped around the abdomen to form a kind of skirt.

Mahābhārata [mahAA bhAA rata]: the great epic poem of India about the struggles between a warring family of princes and the triumph of righteousness.

mahāsamādhi [mahAA sam AAdhi]: a term meaning "the great absorption in the Absolute" which is used to describe the moment a great being leaves his or her body and merges forever with the Truth. It is not an ordinary death. The power and presence of these great beings pervades the universe and can be experienced very strongly even after they have left their bodies.

mālā [maa laa]: in yoga, a *mālā* is a necklace or bracelet strung with auspicious beads and used for repeating the mantra as you touch each bead. Also known as a *japa mālā.*

mantra: a group of letters or words with divine power; a name of God. God in the form of sound.

Mata: ("mother") a respectful way to address an older Indian woman.

meditation: the stilling or calming of the thoughts of the mind in order to attain inner peace and union with God.

mūrti [mOOr ti]: a statue which has been filled with the breath of life during a special ceremony performed by brahmin priests. After this ceremony, the statue is no longer considered inert, but is treated as a living image.

Muslim: one who follows the religion or law of Islam, the spiritual path laid down by Muhammad in the sixth century A.D.

Narada [nAA ra da]: a great and learned saint and prophet, who wrote the *Bhakti Sūtras,* a classical work on the path of devotion, or *bhakti yoga.* He was a devoted servant of Lord Vishnu.

Navaratri [nava rAA tri]: the nine-day festival of worship of the Devi, or Goddess.

Om: the very first sound from which all sound originates. It is the inner essence of all mantras.

Om Namah Shivāya [Om na maa shi vAA ya]: ("salutations to Shiva") the mantra of the Siddha Yoga lineage. Shiva signifies the inner Self. The mantra has the power to protect the one who repeats it.

pādukā(s) [pAA du kaa]: sacred sandals or shoes of the Guru; they carry the Guru's *shakti.*

Pandharpur: a city in Maharashtra, India, which is the main place of pilgrimage for devotees of Lord Vitthal, a form of Lord Krishna.

Paramahamsa [pAra ma hAm sa]: (*parama* means "supreme," *hamsa* means "swan") the Indian scriptures say that the *hamsa,* the swan, has such clarity it can separate milk from water. Also, it can soar very high in the sky, and no matter where it is, it remains a pure being. That is why a true Guru is referred to as a Paramahamsa.

prasād [pra sAAd]: a blessed gift; often refers to food that has first been offered to God and is later distributed.

pūjā [pOO jaa]: an altar with holy images and objects of worship where one prays and makes offerings. Also, the act of worshiping and making offerings.

pyre: a pile of wood or other material used for burning. It is known as a funeral pyre when used for burning a dead body.

Rāmāyana [raa mAA yana]: the oldest of the Sanskrit epic poems; said to be written by the sage Valmiki. It celebrates the life and adventures of Lord Rama. In the story, Sita, Rama's wife, was kidnapped by the ten-headed demon king Ravana. Eventually she was rescued by Lord Rama, along with the help of Hanuman, the monkey god, his loyal monkey subjects, and a kingdom of bears. Rama and Sita then returned triumphantly to their kingdom of Ayodhya where Lord Rama ruled for many years.

Rudra [ru drA]: another name for Lord Shiva: the remover of worldly pain and the lord of destruction (of ego) are two descriptions by which he is known.

rudrāksha beads [ru drAA ksha]: seeds from a tree sacred to Lord Rudra, often strung as beads for *mālās* to be used for mantra repetition.

Rudram [ru drAm]: a chant sung in praise of Lord Shiva. Chanting these verses is considered to be very beneficial for clarity and purity of mind.

rupee: the main denomination of money of India.

sādhana [sAA dha na]: a spiritual path; the practices of spiritual discipline.

sahasrāra [sa has rAAra]: the highest center of subtle energy located at the crown of the head. When this center is pierced by the *kundalinī shakti,* complete union with God takes place.

Sai Baba of Shirdi: a great Siddha who lived in Shirdi, a town in Maharashtra, who had many followers from different religions.

Sanskrit: the ancient and sacred language of India. Sanskrit was first heard by sages during deep meditation and then a written script was developed.

saptah [sap ta]: a continuous chant, often lasting for seven days.

sari: a long piece of fabric (usually cotton or silk) worn by Indian women. It wraps around the body full length, with one end traditionally draped over the head or over one shoulder.

Self: divine Consciousness living in each human being.

seva: see *guruseva.*

shakti [shak tI]: spiritual power or energy, also known as *kundalinī shakti,* the feminine, creative power of the universe.

shaktipāt [shak ti pAAt]: ("descent of grace") the spiritual awakening of the *kundalinī* energy in a disciple by the Guru's grace.

shivalingam [shi va lIng am]: Shiva's sacred symbol; an oval-shaped object representing Shiva, made of stone, metal, or clay.

Shiva, Lord: a name for the Supreme Reality that exists everywhere. Also, in the Hindu trinity, Lord Shiva represents God as the one who destroys ignorance in all forms.

Shivo'ham [shi vO ham]: ("I am Shiva") a Sanskrit mantra which emphasizes that God and the one who repeats the mantra are the same.

Siddha [sid dha]: a perfected yogi; one who has become enlightened or one with God.

Siddha Yoga [sid dha yO ga]: the spiritual path and teachings of the Siddhas as taught by Swami Muktananda. The process begins with the awakening of the *kundalinī* energy in the seeker by the grace of a Siddha Guru, and continues until the process is complete and the disciple has become one with God.

Swami or **Swamiji** [swa mEE jEE]: a respectful way of addressing a *sannyāsi,* or monk.

tamboura: a stringed musical instrument from the lute family. It comes from the East and has a round body and a long neck.

trident: the three-pronged weapon that Shiva is pictured as holding. He also uses it as a pointer, directing people toward the spiritual path.

Vedas: ("knowledge") the four ancient, divinely revealed Indian scriptures. They are the *Rig Veda, Yajur Veda, Sama Veda,* and *Atharva Veda.*

Vedic: refers to the Vedas.

Vishnu: the supreme Lord. Also, in the Hindu trinity, Lord Vishnu represents God as the preserver of all creation.

Vishnu Sahasranāma [vIsh nu sahas ra nAAma]: a Sanskrit chant sung in praise of Lord Vishnu.

Vitthal [vit thal]: a form of Lord Krishna. Lord Krishna went to the house of Pundalik, who was caring for his aged parents. He asked Lord Krishna to wait and threw Him a brick to stand on. The Lord was deeply moved by Pundalik's devotion to his parents and patiently waited. The image of Krishna standing on the brick became known as Vitthal.

wireless station: a radio; telegraph or telephone that doesn't need connection by wire.

Yamuna [ya mU nAA]: a holy river in North India on the banks of which Lord Krishna spent his youth.

Yeola: a village in the state of Maharashtra where Baba spent many years during his *sādhana.*

yoga: the state of union with the Self, or God; also, the practices leading to that state.

yogi: one who practices yoga; also, one who has attained perfection, or Self-realization, through the practices of yoga.

yogini: a female who practices yoga; also one who has attained perfection, or Self-realization, through the practices of yoga.

You may learn more about the teachings and
practices of Siddha Yoga Meditation by contacting:

SYDA Foundation
371 Brickman Rd.
P.O. Box 600
South Fallsburg, NY 12779-0600, USA

Tel: (914) 434-2000

or

Gurudev Siddha Peeth
P.O. Ganeshpuri
PIN 401 206
District Thana
Maharashtra, India

For further information about books in print by Swami Muktananda and
Swami Chidvilasananda, and editions in translation, please contact:

Siddha Yoga Meditation Bookstore
371 Brickman Rd.
P.O. Box 600
South Fallsburg, NY 12779-0600, USA

Tel: (914) 434-2000 ext. 1700